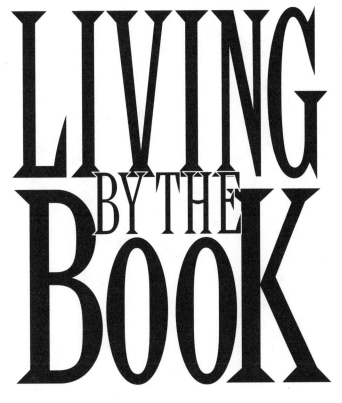

LIVING BY THE BOOK

WORKBOOK

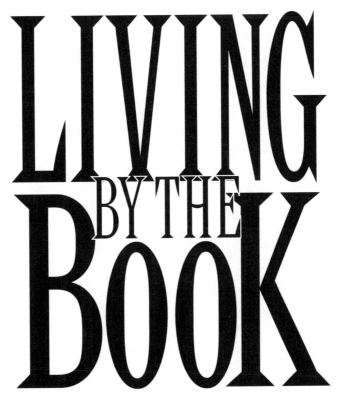

LIVING BY THE BOOK

WORKBOOK

LIVING BY THE BOOK

WORKBOOK

HOWARD G. HENDRICKS
WILLIAM D. HENDRICKS

MOODY PRESS

CHICAGO

MOODY PRESS
CHICAGO

© 2000 by
HOWARD G. HENDRICKS
WILLIAM D. HENDRICKS

All Scripture quotations, unless indicated, are taken from the *New American Standard Bible®*, Copyright © 1960, 1962, 1963, 1968, 1971, 1972, 1973, 1975, 1977, and 1995 by The Lockman Foundation. Used by permission.

Scripture quotations marked (NIV) are taken from the *Holy Bible: New International Version®*. NIV®. Copyright © 1973, 1978, 1984 by International Bible Society. Used by permission of Zondervan Publishing House. All rights reserved.

The "NIV" and "New International Version" trademarks are registered in the United States Patent and Trademark Office by International Bible Society. Use of either trademark requires permission of International Bible Society.

Occasional quotations from *Living by the Book,* © 1991 by Howard G. Hendricks and William D. Hendricks, are by permission of the publisher, Moody Press, Moody Bible Institute of Chicago.

ISBN: 0-8024-9532-X

5 7 9 10 8 6

Printed in the United States of America

Contents

Part 2

Interpretation

From Observation to Interpretation

Part 3
Application

From Interpretation to Application

Part 4
Putting It All Together

Introduction

Acknowledgements

To Stan Campbell, a very capable editor and writer, who shaped this manuscript and based the exercises and sequence upon the original work, *Living By The Book*. Many thanks for your fine work.

Preface

When *Living by the Book* was published in 1991, our intent as authors was to help people learn good Bible study methods that would help them observe, interpret, and apply Scripture. It seems that many people run into problems along this process, resulting in a lot of erroneous and inappropriate interpretation and practice of biblical teaching. We hoped to provide a methodical system of approaching God's Word—one that would let Scripture speak clearly to the reader. It's a system that I (Howard) have taught in my years at Dallas Theological Seminary, and we felt it would be helpful to others as well.

Apparently the book met a need for many people. Now, almost a decade later, our publisher has asked us to follow up the original text with this workbook. We were glad to do so. While the first book focused on the learning process, this one allows you to do more implementation and integration of those principles.

We realize the problem of releasing a workbook almost a decade after the original text. Some of you may have problems securing copies of *Living by the Book*. Others may have read the book years ago, but could use a refresher course. Perhaps you've even loaned your book to someone who apparently liked it so much that it never found its way back to you.

No matter. While we certainly encourage you to read *Living by the Book* prior to beginning this workbook, that isn't mandatory. You'll find many references to the original material throughout this workbook, but we've tried to provide you with the essentials of the book in bits and pieces throughout this work. For example, each day's assignment contains an insert from *Living by the Book*, along with a page reference. If you are clear about what to do, you can move forward with boldness. But if you need clarification or more of a review, you can consult the book before completing that portion of the workbook.

Bible study doesn't require a high IQ or long hours of intensive toil. You'll discover that a few minutes each day using an effective learning process will reveal much new insight. Learning and retaining Scripture works much the same way as studying for a subject in school. It's more effective to develop a regular habit of study than to try to "cram" for a couple of days and then do nothing for the rest of the week.

Speaking of school, you might consider going through this workbook with a group. If you form your own "class," you tend to be accountable to one another in addition to being able to draw from others' observations, interpretations, and applications. If you can't get a group together on a regular basis, perhaps you can find a single "study partner." You can benefit greatly from having someone with whom you can discuss what you're learning. (See chapter 45 of *Living by the Book* for more specific suggestions.)

Also keep in mind that this workbook is only a guideline for your study. It follows the process described in *Living by the Book*. But never forget that this is for *your* benefit. If you want to take longer, skip around, add your own pages, replace suggested Scripture passages, etc., then that's up to you.

This workbook goes through the entire *Living by the Book* process, after which you will find two complete Bible studies—one on the Book of Ruth and another on the Book of James. In these Bible book studies, we've tried to demonstrate how to integrate the methods you've learned while still following the Observation, Interpretation, and Application process.

We hope you'll come to find Bible study as thrilling and applicable as we do. The Word of God is still "living and active" (Hebrews 4:12). Our prayer is that it will come alive in *your* life.

HOWARD G. HENDRICKS
WILLIAM D. HENDRICKS

Part 1

OBSERVATION

START WITH OBSERVATION

Let us begin by reemphasizing the importance of observing Scripture before attempting to interpret or apply it. Most of the activities in this workbook will involve learning to see what the Bible really says. Only then is it prudent to begin to try to make sense of it.

A police detective would never be content to allow eyewitnesses to phone in their statements in a murder case without going to check out the crime scene firsthand. He or she would want to *observe* the scene and take in every little detail—both to better understand what happened and to ensure that what he or she is being told is the truth. Similarly, we must learn to interact with Scripture on our own. Sermons are good and commentaries can be helpful, but both are someone else's interpretations of what the Bible says. If we truly believe the Bible is God's Word, we need to patiently observe it and learn to let it speak to us—individually and personally.

Through Observation we learn to get beyond the obvious. We begin to see the importance of little words and phrases that are easily missed at first glance. We pay attention to things that might be repeated or emphasized. We put ourselves in the place of the person being described so that we can better understand what he or she might be experiencing. And as we continue to observe, we begin to see much more clearly what God is saying to us.

So the next several exercises will take you through the process of Observation. We think you'll find a few pleasant surprises as you go along.

1
OBSERVING A PASSAGE OF SCRIPTURE

W hat makes one person a better Bible student than another? He can see more, that's all. The same truth is available to both of them in the text" (p. 47).

If you want to get more out of Bible study, it helps to know what you're looking for. Use the following list of questions to help guide you in your search of Scripture. You probably won't use every question for each passage you study, but at least they provide a good starting point. The more completely you can answer these questions, the better you will observe God's truth, which then provides a strong foundation for Interpretation and Application.

- Who is the author of the passage?
- Whom is the author addressing? (God's people? A specific church? Unbelievers?)
- What is the most important term and/or concept of the passage?
- What are the main verbs? What is the verb tense?
- Are there terms you need to define so you can better understand the passage?
- Are there people or places you need to identify?
- What do you already know about the people and places mentioned?
- Can you identify any cause-effect relationships in the author's writing?
- In what ways does the passage apply to your own personal life? (If there isn't a clear application, is there a more subtle one?)
- What things from this passage might you want to study later in further detail?

NOTE You might want to make a copy of this page to place in each of the Bibles you use.

2

OBSERVING
A VERSE

TODAY'S PASSAGE
Psalm 93:1

TIME COMMITMENT:
30 minutes

Remember, in Observation your main concern is, What do I see? Pay special attention to terms and grammatical structure. Also look at the context" (p. 63).

Let's try observing Psalm 93:1. Since we're choosing a psalm, the context of what comes before and afterward may not be as important as in a narrative passage. However, the more you read the Psalms, the better you can detect similarities and contrasts.

But for now let's turn our attention to this single verse:

"The Lord reigns, He is clothed with majesty; the Lord has clothed and girded Himself with strength; indeed, the world is firmly established, it will not be moved."

Begin by going through the questions on the "Observing a Passage of Scripture" sheet. Not all of them will apply, of course. But you can note the grammatical tense. If the psalmist wrote in present tense, does that mean the verse is now past tense?

_____

_____

What would you say is the main theme of this verse?

_____

_____

Forget about religious language for a moment. What then comes to mind when you think about a "lord"?

_____

In addition to the questions already provided, here are a few additional things to observe to get you started:

- What words or phrases are repeated? Why do you suppose they are so emphasized?

"clothed" with majesty and strength. Being clothed is like being fully encased.

- God is described by the terms "majesty" and "strength." What connection, if any, do these terms have? (Does one necessarily suggest the other?)

- Why did the author suddenly move from describing "the Lord" to writing about "the world"?

The Lord made the world and he reigns over it.

- We all know the earth is turning on its axis. So what does it mean that the world "will not be moved"?

Its foundations, being created by a perfect God, will not be moved.

- Does this verse evoke any positive feelings for you?

The feeling that the Lord reigns and he's in charge so I don't have to worry.

- Might this verse cause less positive emotions for some people (fear, anxiety, etc.)?

Yes it could if God is a scary concept.

What other observations can you make from this single verse?

3

OBSERVING
A VERSE

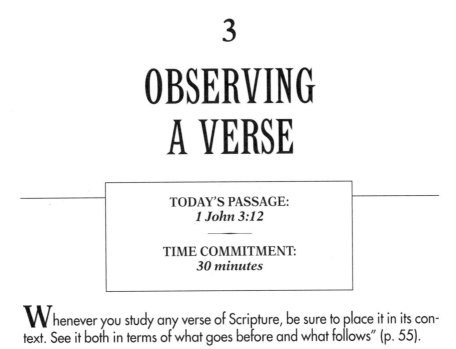

TODAY'S PASSAGE:
1 John 3:12

TIME COMMITMENT:
30 minutes

Whenever you study any verse of Scripture, be sure to place it in its context. See it both in terms of what goes before and what follows" (p. 55).

First John 3:12 should provide ample opportunity for you to practice your observation skills. Here is the verse, with space provided for your notations:

"not as Cain, who was of the evil one, and slew his brother. And for what reason did he slay him? Because his deeds were evil, and his brother's were righteous."

Here are a few suggestions:

- Again, begin by using the questions on the "Observing a Passage of Scripture" sheet. This time you should find more significance in the author, the context, and the people mentioned. (Regarding context, any time a verse begins in midsentence, you have a clear mandate to take note of what precedes it.)

_____

_____

- Read the story the writer refers to (Genesis 4:1–16). What new insight does this shed on the verse?

_____

_____

- Determine why this verse is dropped into the center of a chapter focusing on God's love.

_____

- Try to think of examples in your own life in which you see a contrast between righteous and evil actions and the consequences that result.

_____

_____

- When, in your own life, have you acted as Cain did (to a lesser extent)? When have you suffered as Abel did? How does this verse speak to each of those situations?

_____

_____

What other observations can you make about this verse?

_____

_____

_____

_____

4

READING THE BIBLE
AS FOR THE FIRST TIME

> **TODAY'S PASSAGE:**
> *(See below)*
>
> **TIME COMMITMENT:**
> *30 minutes*

It helps to read the Bible in different versions. If you've been reading the same translation for years, try something fresh and contemporary for a change" (p. 67).

Today's assignment might require a trip to the library or a nearby Christian bookstore. Or perhaps you can borrow some Bibles from friends or your church. But be prepared to find several different translations/paraphrases of the Bible to read and compare.

One of the best ways to read the Bible as for the first time is to look up portions of Scripture that are most familiar to you. But if you don't have a particular passage in mind, try one or more of the following:

- The creation story (Genesis 2:4–25)
- Psalm 23
- A prophecy about the coming Messiah (such as Isaiah 9:6–7)
- The Beatitudes (Matthew 5:1–12)
- Paul's conversion (Acts 9:1–19)

Select one or more passages and read the same account from four different Bible versions. Some readings are likely to be quite similar. But if you contrast the King James Version with *The Living Bible,* for example, be prepared for a significant difference. In each case, try to put aside what you already know and let the text speak to you freshly, as if it were the first time you were reading it.

NOTE any discoveries or insights in the space below.

5

READING THE BIBLE AS FOR THE FIRST TIME

TODAY'S PASSAGE:
Luke 15:11–32

TIME COMMITMENT:
30 minutes

It is often said that familiarity breeds contempt. Well, something else it breeds is ignorance. The moment you come to a passage of Scripture and say, 'Oh, I know this one already,' you're in trouble. Instead you need to come to every text as if you'd never seen it before in your life" (p. 67).

Frequently the passages that are most in danger of being overlooked are those that are most familiar. So let's take a look at one of the best-known portions of the Bible: the parable of the prodigal son. It's found in Luke 15:11–32.

Read the parable as if you were an eight year old hearing the story for the first time. What questions or comments would you have?

_____

_____

Read it again from the following perspectives, each time noting the questions you might be likely to ask:

- A person from a foreign country (and different religious culture) hearing this story for the first time

_____

_____

- A person who is skeptical about the authority of the Bible

_____

_____

- A parent whose child has rebelled and left home

_____

_____

- Someone who has allowed the harsh situations of life to distance him or her from God

_____

_____

As you read through the eyes of these various people, the text might reveal a number of fresh insights you had not yet noticed.

_____

_____

_____

_____

6

READING THE BIBLE AS A LOVE LETTER

TODAY'S PASSAGE:
Isaiah 55

———

TIME COMMITMENT:
30 minutes

T he way to come to the Word of God [is to] read it as though it were His love letter to you" (p. 69).

Sometimes we perceive the writings of the prophets to be some of the least "loving" of the Scriptures. The prophets brought messages from God, and much of what they had to say pointed to what people could expect as the consequences of their sins. But God also sprinkled the prophetic books with promises and reasons for confident hope among His people.

Isaiah wrote to alert the people of Judah that they would eventually be taken into captivity by the Babylonians. Much of what he had to say was harsh, direct, and to the point. But equally to the point was what they could expect *beyond* their captivity.

Put yourself in the place of someone who had been carried away by an enemy army, or left amid the ruins of a once-grand city. You would remember that Isaiah had warned about such a future, but you might also recall something else. Your world is crumbling around you as you locate a scroll containing Isaiah 55. Read the text, then consider the following questions.

- How would you feel upon reading this passage, in light of your present sufferings?

_____

_____

- What would this text tell you about God?

_____

_____

- What would be your attitude about the future?

_____

_____

As you look back to see God's involvement with His people in the past, what can you determine about your own future?

_____

_____

_____

_____

Assignment for another day:

It's a simple matter to note the depth of God's love in such passages as Isaiah 55. A greater challenge is to learn to detect His love in passages that forecast judgment and suffering. However, if God's nature does not change, wouldn't it be true that God's discipline of sin is motivated by love just as is His outpouring of blessing? The next time you read a somber passage of Scripture, try to determine how God's love is active even during such times.

7

READING THE BIBLE AS A LOVE LETTER

TODAY'S PASSAGE:
John 3:16–17

———

TIME COMMITMENT:
30 minutes

Just think of it: God wanted to communicate with you in the twentieth century—and He wrote His message in a Book" (p. 70).

Surely the most quoted Scripture reference about God's love is John 3:16. Yet it can be interpreted quite impersonally if we don't get specific about it. Below is John 3:16–17:

"For God so loved the world, that He gave His only begotten Son, that whoever believes in Him shall not perish, but have eternal life. For God did not send the Son into the world to judge the world, but that the world might be saved through Him."

Instead of thinking about "the world," let's get personal and substitute some specific names. In order to do so, here's the verse again with some blanks. It's up to you to fill in the blanks with the names that follow.

"For God so loved _____, that He gave His only begotten Son, that whoever believes in Him shall not perish, but have eternal life. For God did not send the Son to _____ to judge _____, but that _____ might be saved through Him."

Try substituting some of these names into the previous passage:

Your boss	A difficult child	A neighbor
A coworker	Someone at church	Someone from your past
Your spouse	Your own name	A personal enemy

Do you think God's love for the previous people is any more or less than it is for you? Explain.

If you were to see other people as God sees them, do you think you would need to make changes in any of your relationships? Why?

_____

_____

_____

If you personalize John 3:16–17, the passage takes on a much more intimate feel. The same is true about many other portions of the Bible. If the love of God toward us is not clearly evident, we're probably not looking hard enough.

8

READING THOUGHTFULLY

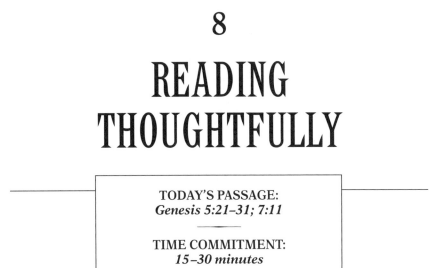

TODAY'S PASSAGE:
Genesis 5:21–31; 7:11

TIME COMMITMENT:
15–30 minutes

The step of observation requires you to assume the role of a biblical detective, searching for clues as to the meaning of the text" (p. 77).

Today's reading is from one of the "begats" sections of Scripture—the portions we tend to skip over. However, there are some noteworthy people mentioned in this passage. Noah is the most familiar. But in his family tree are a couple of other names you should know.

Methuselah would have been in the *Guinness Book of World Records* if it had existed at this time. Figure out your year of birth if you were 969 years old today. Based on the changes that have taken place since that year, can you gain any insight into the kind of person Methuselah might have been (provided that his mind was still sharp at his age)?

_____

_____

Enoch is another name you need to know. What is significant about his life (5:21–24)?

_____

_____

But you don't have to read very thoughtfully to make these simple observations. If you read closely, like a detective, you might by now be asking yourself, Did Methuselah die in the flood? Figure it out for yourself:

How old was Methuselah when Lamech was born? (5:25) _____
How old was Lamech when Noah was born? (5:28) _____
How old was Noah when the flood came? (7:11) _____

If you add the numbers, you should get Methuselah's age at the time of the great flood. _____

By reading thoughtfully, you discover that Methuselah died in the year of the flood. We can't say whether or not he died as a result of the flood, but it raises questions. His father, Enoch, walked with God to the point that he hadn't literally died like everyone else. Had Methuselah's life also been a good one—long and full, and ending just prior to the flood? Or had he turned away from God and his father's faith, drowning with the rest of the wicked people who caused God's heart to be "filled with pain" (Genesis 6:6 NIV)?

_____

_____

_____

_____

We don't always discover the answers to all our questions, but by reading thoughtfully we at least begin to ask better questions about the depth and mysteries of Scripture.

9

READING THOUGHTFULLY

TODAY'S PASSAGE:
Luke 17:11–19

———

TIME COMMITMENT:
30 – 60 minutes

When you come to the Bible, put your thinking cap on. Don't throw your mind into neutral. Apply the same mental discipline that you would to any subject in which you take a vital interest" (p. 77).

How would you reply to someone who asked, "If I do exactly as God instructs me, will He be pleased with me?"

Most of us would agree that obedience pleases God, yet a familiar passage of Scripture sheds some light on this assumption. You probably know the story of Jesus and the ten lepers. But have you ever read the account thoughtfully?

Read Luke 17:11–19 and think about the story for several minutes before answering the following questions.

- What did the lepers ask Jesus to do?

_____

_____

- What was the underlying desire behind their request?

_____

_____

- What did Jesus tell the lepers to do?

_____

_____

- How many lepers did exactly as He instructed?

_____

_____

- The Samaritan leper broke ranks and returned to Jesus. Why?

_____

_____

- Why did Jesus express dismay about the other nine (seemingly obedient) lepers?

_____

_____

Based on a thoughtful consideration of this story, do you think God is always pleased with our unquestioned obedience? Why or why not?

_____

_____

_____

What would you say is a lesson we could learn from this account?

_____

_____

_____

10
READING REPEATEDLY

TODAY'S PASSAGE:
Exodus 20:1–21

———

TIME COMMITMENT:
30 minutes daily

T he genius of the Word of God is that it has staying power; it can stand up to repeated exposure. In fact, that's why it is unlike any other book" (p. 81).

So you think you know the Ten Commandments? Let's spend a week as you read them repeatedly each day, and perhaps you'll gather some new insights into this familiar passage.

Day 1 Before reading the passage, see how many of the Ten Commandments you can recall from memory. (The national average is three to four.) Then read Exodus 20:1–21 to see how well you did. Spend some time thinking about what you've already been taught about this passage from books, sermons, etc.

_____

_____

_____

Day 2 Read the book of Exodus from the beginning until you get to Exodus 20. What is the significance of the Ten Commandments in light of the events just preceding them?

_____

_____

_____

LIVING BY THE BOOK

Day 3 Put yourself in the place of an Israelite standing at the foot of Mount Sinai after being led out of slavery in Egypt. You would be hearing these commandments for the first time. How do you think you would feel? Why?

_____

_____

_____

Day 4 Read Exodus 20:1–21 in one or more alternative Bible translations. What differences do you notice as you do?

_____

_____

_____

Day 5 If possible, find a cassette recording of the Ten Commandments. In lieu of that, read Exodus 20:1–21 aloud. Remember that this is the way the Israelites first learned of these instructions. Do you prefer a verbal or a written presentation of Scripture? Why?

_____

_____

_____

Day 6 Read Exodus 20:1–21 again. This time try to determine if the order of the commandments is significant. (Are they prioritized? Can you determine groupings among the existing list? If you mixed them up, would they be just as effective? Etc.)

_____

_____

_____

Day 7 Read Exodus 20:1–21 for a final time. But don't move on until you discover three things you haven't yet noticed.

_____

_____

_____

NOTE Many versions of Scripture are now available on-line. You can key in the passage you're looking for and download a variety of translations or paraphrases.

11
READING REPEATEDLY

TODAY'S PASSAGE:
Romans 5

———

TIME COMMITMENT:
30 minutes daily

Y ou may be an expert in a given field. If you read a book in that field two or three times, you've got it. You can put it on the shelf and move on to something else. But that's never true of the Bible. Read it over and over again, and you'll still see things that you've never seen before" (p. 81).

Certain passages of Scripture almost demand repeated readings, and the book of Romans contains many such examples. Plan to spend the next week thinking about Romans 5.

Day 1 Read Romans 5. Spend a half hour or so differentiating between the portions you think you understand clearly and those that may remain something of a mystery to you. Record any questions you have.

_____

_____

_____

Day 2 To put Romans 5 in a proper context, read Romans 1–5 straight through. As you read Romans 5 again, make a note of any verses that refer back to something Paul had already said in Romans 1–4. [Note: Any passage that begins with "Therefore" will refer to previous material.]

_____

_____

_____

Day 3 If possible, find an audio version of this passage. (Other options include having someone else read it to you, or reading it aloud.) Listen for repeated words or phrases. What is Paul trying to emphasize in this passage?

_____

_____

_____

Day 4 Paul is dealing with some complex issues and deep thoughts. Use one or more different translations to try to get some alternative ways to express his statements. (You might want to try the Phillips translation, which inserts clarifying statements within the text.)

_____

_____

_____

Day 5 Go to the other extreme from what you did yesterday. Today try to find a simplified paraphrase of Romans 5. Consider the *New Living Translation, The Message,* or even a children's translation. Determine how these concepts might be explained to people who don't have a vast understanding of Scripture.

_____

_____

_____

Day 6 Suppose you're a reporter and Romans 5 is an account that comes in over the wires. It's your job to write it up. Read the chapter again. Then determine what you think should be the headline and lead sentence.

_____

_____

_____

Day 7 Read Romans 5 again. Have any of your questions from Day 1 been answered by now? If you have remaining questions, good! Perhaps you'll keep reading until they are clarified. If you don't give up, you will arrive at answers to most of your Bible questions.

_____

_____

_____

12

READING
PATIENTLY

The fruit of the Word takes time to ripen. So if you are the least bit impatient, you're liable to bail out early and miss a rich harvest" (p. 87).

For this and the next exercise on "reading patiently," feel free to take some liberties with what we're suggesting. After all, these Bible studies are for your benefit.

If you'd rather tackle a different passage than the one suggested, please do so. We're recommending you spend a month examining the same text. If you're ready to move on in three weeks, go ahead. If you're still going strong after two months, good for you!

But in all the variety and leeway we hope you enjoy, we *would* like to remain firm that you maintain a commitment to use only your Bible during most of this exercise. While secondary sources will certainly have much to offer, the most significant gains come from your own personal interaction with Scripture. It's OK to struggle a bit and have unanswered questions. While you may continue to not understand all that you are reading, you'll still be making new discoveries every day.

You may not want to do the Old Testament and New Testament assignments consecutively. It's perfectly acceptable to spend a month or so with one of them, move ahead with other exercises in this workbook, and come back to the other when you're ready for another opportunity to read patiently. You might even want to postpone this exercise until you go through the workbook and try the Bible studies that follow. (You can spend a month in the book of Ruth and/or the book of James after going through the Observation, Interpretation, and Application process.) At this point, however, we're still in the initial stages of Observation. If you're spending a month in a single book, you should be doing so to observe everything you can.

> **OLD TESTAMENT STUDY FOR A MONTH:**
> *The book of Malachi*
>
> **NEW TESTAMENT STUDY FOR A MONTH:**
> *The book of 1 John*
>
> ---
>
> **TIME COMMITMENT:**
> *About 30 minutes daily*

There's a vast difference between running sprints and running cross-country. To do the latter you need to develop the kicker, the second wind. You've got to prepare for the long haul. So it is with patient Bible reading. You have to develop some stamina, some staying power to hang on with a text until you start to make some progress" (p. 88).

As you begin your one-month study of your chosen assignment, first "zoom out" and read the passage (or book) in one sitting to get an overview for what you will be learning. Make sure you continue to see the "big picture" of the passage. But then "zoom in" and spend a few days focused on some of the specifics. For instance:

- What can you learn about the author—his character, opinions, writing style, and so forth?
- For whom is the book written? In what ways do you tend to relate to that particular audience?
- What does the author have to say about the past? Present? Future?
- What warnings are contained in the text, either blatant or implied?
- What promises are made to the reader?
- What does the author want the reader(s) to do?
- What, if any, teachings are unique to the author? Which ones seem to echo the teachings of other Bible writers?
- What, if anything, is noteworthy about the writing style (grammar, sentence structure, word choices, use of metaphors/similes, repetition, and so on)?
- What other observations do you feel are significant?

The keys to reading the Bible patiently are: Be patient with the text, and be patient with yourself. . . . So as you dive into the Word for yourself, relax and enjoy the experience. God's truth is there, and you'll find it if you just give yourself time to read patiently" (p. 90).

13

READING SELECTIVELY

TODAY'S PASSAGE:
Genesis 11:27–12:9

———

TIME COMMITMENT:
30 minutes

Selective Bible reading involves using the right bait when you troll the Scriptures. Here are six "lures" that you can use with any text, six questions to ask any passage of Scripture. . . . Who are the people involved? What is happening in this paragraph? Where is it taking place? When is it taking place? Why do you think God put it in the narrative? And what difference would this make in your life?" (pp. 91, 95–96).

The call of Abraham to leave his homeland and travel to Canaan is familiar to many people. We find it admirable that Abraham was so faithful and obedient. Yet many people have never read this account selectively. If we apply our set of six questions to this passage, we may find a new level of respect for Abraham's obedience to God.

Read Genesis 11:27–12:9. Then refer back to the passage as you answer the following questions.

- Who are the people mentioned in this passage?

_____

_____

- What is happening?

_____

_____

- Where is the action taking place? (You may need a Bible map to track the various locations mentioned in this passage.)

_____

- When does this event take place? Don't worry so much about determining a precise year. More importantly, determine its significance in the flow of Bible history. (In this case, the last major story is found in Genesis 11:1–9—an account that emphasizes God's desire for people to "scatter" over the face of the whole earth.)

- Why do you think God put this story in the Bible? (Why begin with Terah rather than Abraham? Why mention all those family members and Abraham's comfortable home in Ur? Why mention Sarah's infertility as soon as her name comes up?)

- Finally, since God *did* include this account in Scripture, what are we supposed to learn from it? What does this bit of ancient history have to do with your life today?

By reading selectively, do you notice more of a family attachment that you might not have seen before? Not only did Abraham follow God's call to a new land, he followed God's call to "leave . . . your people and your father's household" (Genesis 12:1 NIV). Many people will follow God's call when it's convenient to do so, but far fewer are willing to place God above the comforts of home and the security of a strong family bond. Abraham did both, and was eventually rewarded (tremendously!) for doing so.

14

READING
SELECTIVELY

TODAY'S PASSAGE:
Matthew 2:1–12; Luke 2:1–40

TIME COMMITMENT:
30 minutes

Y̶ou may wonder, why does God clutter the biblical text with this sort of stuff? Why so many inane, off-the-wall comments and details? The reason is because He wants you to see the process people went through in order to come to the conclusions they came to" (p. 92).

The Christmas story. We hear it every December and know it so well we hardly listen to it anymore. But let's examine it like any other portion of Scripture and see what we can learn by reading it selectively. Read Matthew 2:1–12 and Luke 2:1–40. Then answer these questions.

- Who are the people involved? Record the "minor characters" as well as the familiar ones.

_____

_____

- What is happening in these passages? By what various means is God working?

_____

_____

- Where is the action taking place? (If you were going to create a play out of this story, how many sets would you need?)

_____

_____

- When is it taking place? (Again, the year may not be as significant as knowing what's happening during this particular historical era.)

_____

_____

- Why do you think God put this story in the biblical narrative? (Why not just begin with Jesus' baptism and public ministry?)

_____

_____

- What difference should this story make in your life? (Is it just a warm account of the first Christmas, or is God trying to tell us something?)

_____

_____

HINT With the large roster of people involved in the birth of the baby Jesus, might this first Christmas be an example of the wide inclusion of people Jesus would later call to Himself as an adult? If so, how?

_____

_____

_____

_____

15

READING PRAYERFULLY

TODAY'S PASSAGE:
Jonah 2

———

TIME COMMITMENT:
30 – 60 minutes

W e tend to think of Bible study and prayer as separate disciplines, but the fact is, they are integrally related. Prayer is really a key to effective Bible study. Lean to pray before, during, and after your reading of the Scriptures" (p. 97).

Begin today's assignment by spending time in prayer, telling God what you hope to accomplish from this Bible study and asking Him to show you what He wants you to know.

Read Jonah 2 straight through.

Read the same passage again, this time pausing to think of your own situations that may be somewhat comparable to Jonah's. As they come to mind, stop to ask for God's guidance in dealing with each one.

Read through Jonah 2 a third time. This time use the observational skills you have already learned. For example:

- What do you find significant about this prayer based on the context of where it is taking place?

_____

_____

- What can you discover about prayer based on Jonah's setting? His honesty? His state of mind? His willingness to learn from his experience and change?

_____

_____

- What does this prayer tell you about Jonah? What does it tell you about God?

_____

_____

- How do you think Jonah's life might have been different if he had stopped to pray before finding himself in this predicament?

_____

_____

Conclude today's study with a time of prayer (1) to thank God for seeing you through the rough spots in life, and (2) to commit yourself to Him in obedience as you face future trials.

16

READING PRAYERFULLY

TODAY'S PASSAGE:
Ephesians 3

———

TIME COMMITMENT:
30–60 minutes

Of all the strategies to first-rate Bible reading, prayerful reading proba-bly requires the most cultivation" (p. 101).

Ephesians 3 is part of a letter where we might say that Paul was *writing* prayerfully. As Paul considered all God was doing for himself and others, he was moved to include a prayer for the Ephesians within the letter itself. We can maintain a prayerful mind-set as we *read* this letter.

First read Ephesians 3:1–13. Consider:

- What were some of the things on Paul's mind for which he was thankful?

_____

_____

- What "mystery" was being uncovered for which the Ephesians (and we) should be grateful?

_____

_____

- Based on this information, how did Paul want the Ephesians (and us) to respond?

_____

_____

Read Paul's prayer in Ephesians 3:14–21. This particular prayer doesn't contain much *confession* on Paul's part (though he is very clear about his past sins in other portions of Scripture).

- What *adoration* does Paul include in his prayer?

_____

_____

- What are Paul's *petitions* to God?

_____

_____

- How do you think it made the Ephesians feel to know that Paul was praying these things on their behalf?

_____

_____

Do you find motivation to pray based on the content of Ephesians 3? If so, consider:

- What specific things do you find for which you can pray with adoration? (Are there any promises to claim?)

_____

_____

- Does anything here prompt a confession for recent actions or thoughts?

_____

_____

- Like Paul, do you know anyone for whom you would like to petition God, praying for the best God has to offer them based on Ephesians 3?

_____

_____

Reading the Bible prayerfully should not only help you get more from Scripture; it should make prayer become much more natural and effective for you. Remember, stop trying to compare your prayers to anyone else's. Prayer is simply communication between you and God. Be yourself, and you'll do much better at seeing God for who He really is.

17

READING IMAGINATIVELY

TODAY'S PASSAGE:
Daniel 6

———

TIME COMMITMENT:
30 – 60 minutes

I t is sad but true that the average person thinks that reading the Bible is dreadfully boring. . . . Yet I'm convinced that the reason Scripture seems dull to so many people is that we come to it dully" (p. 103).

Read Daniel 6 to remind yourself of the facts about this well-known story. Then put your imagination in gear as you read the chapter again—this time trying to put yourself in Daniel's place.

First try to determine how would you feel if you were Daniel. Suppose you have gone out of your way to remain faithful to God in an environment where you're the only godly person. You know how you ought to feel in such a situation, but try to identify how you would really feel if this were happening to you instead of Daniel. For example:

- How would you feel about peers who went out of their way to find you guilty when you had done nothing wrong?

_____

_____

- How would you feel about a boss who claimed to like you, but who wouldn't stand up for you under pressure from the group?

_____

_____

- How would you feel about God's willingness to let you be found guilty and sentenced?

_____

49

- How would you feel about yourself when your faithfulness had apparently gotten you nowhere?

As Daniel was thrown into the lions' den, do you think he had absolute confidence that God would see him through this trial alive?

Do you think he expected to die?

Do you think he might have been the least bit scared?

If you were in Daniel's position, what would you be thinking?

We know that Daniel didn't die; yet try to envision his ordeal. For example:

- He spent the night in the den of lions. Could he even see the big cats, or could he only hear them pacing?

- How do you suppose the place smelled (in the days before kitty litter)?

- How would you have passed the time?

- As hours went by without being mauled, would you grow more confident or more nervous?

Upon your release, would you have been as gracious as Daniel was to the king (vv. 21–22)? How would you have felt about the judgment that was pronounced on your accusers (v. 24)?

These questions are likely to raise others of your own. Learning to read this and other passages imaginatively causes the Bible to come to life more than you might ever expect.

18

READING
IMAGINATIVELY

TODAY'S PASSAGE:
John 2:1–11

TIME COMMITMENT:
30 – 60 minutes

If we always read Scripture in the same way and in the same place time after time, we run the risk of making it into a routine exercise with little interest or excitement. What a tragedy, especially when we consider that history's greatest works of art and music have been created by people who learned to read the Bible imaginatively" (p. 107).

Read John 2:1–11. You probably know the story, but let's try to use our imagination a little bit.

Think back to the last wedding you attended of someone who was close to you. Suppose that person and his or her new spouse showed up at their reception to discover that for some reason there were no beverages. There were expensive canapés and extravagant desserts, but nothing to wash them down with. And all the nearby stores were closed. The newlyweds had no Plan B. How do you suppose they would feel? How would you feel as you saw them in such an embarrassing position on what should be their special day? Do you think everyone would be content to toast them with water?

_____

_____

_____

With that in mind, how do you think Jesus felt when He heard that the newly married couple at Cana was running out of wine for their guests?

_____

_____

Do you feel there is any significance in the fact that this was the first of Jesus' miracles? If so, why?

_____

Do you get the sense that Jesus was concerned only for the spiritual well-being of this couple? What does your response suggest about Jesus' concern for your own current struggles?

_____

_____

_____

If we read this account with little or no imagination, we conclude that Jesus' first miracle was turning water into wine. But if we imagine ourselves there, or Jesus here among us, we may get a glimpse of an infinite God who is concerned about *all* of our problems and embarrassments of life.

Similar lessons are to be found when we use our imagination as we sail with Noah, stand in the fiery furnace, witness the fall of Jerusalem, worship at the manger, or share a plank with Paul after a violent shipwreck.

If your imagination is out of shape, you'll need more practice than most people. But if you're willing to put a little effort into these exercises, we imagine you will benefit immensely.

19
READING MEDITATIVELY

TODAY'S PASSAGE:
2 Samuel 6:1–8

———

TIME COMMITMENT:
At least one day

Use your time—at the beginning of the day, at coffee break, during your lunch hour, riding home from work, before you go to sleep at night—to reflect upon the truth that you study" (p. 113).

You can meditate on any verse or passage of Scripture—and you should. But reading meditatively is perhaps most helpful for the portions of the Bible that may seem unclear or that don't have easy interpretations. We've chosen one such passage for your reading today.

Read 2 Samuel 6:1–8 and look at the questions that follow, but don't answer them yet. Give your mind at least a day to mull over the significance of the story. Think about it as often as possible during the day. Then come back to these questions in a day or so and answer them.

(1) Do you know the context of this story? (If not, skim through the previous chapters of 2 Samuel to see what's going on.)

_____

_____

(2) What kind of guy was Uzzah?

_____

_____

(3) What did Uzzah do that was so wrong? What might have happened if he hadn't acted?

_____

(4) Do you think God's immediate judgment was perhaps too severe? Why or why not?

(5) How might this tragedy have been prevented? (For one suggestion, see Exodus 37:1–5.)

(6) Previously, seventy people had died from looking into the ark (1 Samuel 6:19–20 NIV). Even though Uzzah tried to keep it from falling, he died the moment he touched it. Yet when David had the ark sheltered within a nearby home, the household experienced God's blessing as long as the ark was there. What do these stories suggest about the ark (or about God Himself)?

(7) Do you think this story is more about Uzzah, or about God? Why?

(8) When was the last time you or someone close to you asked, "Why would God allow this to happen?" Can you detect anything from this story that might apply to such situations?

(9) What else do you think we should learn from Uzzah's experience?

20

READING MEDITATIVELY

TODAY'S PASSAGE:
Romans 8:28–39

———

TIME COMMITMENT:
At least one day

Meditation as popularly taught by the Eastern philosophies tells you to empty your mind—the exact opposite of what the Scriptures say. Biblical meditation means filling your mind with the truth that God has revealed. . . . The greatest changes that God has brought about in my life have come through the process of meditation—just allowing the Word of God to filter and percolate through my mind and into my life. I've learned that first-rate Bible reading calls not for snapshots but for timed exposures" (pp. 111, 113).

For this session we've selected an encouraging passage. There's only one question on which to meditate. Today read Romans 8:28–39 and take an advance look at the question. But as before, wait at least a day (or more if you wish) to let your mind dwell on this single passage. When you're ready, come back and answer the question.

Paul made many wonderful promises in this passage. And then he made the observation that "we are more than conquerors" (v. 37 NIV). Your question is: What do you think it means to be "more than conquerors," and how should such a concept affect our lives?

_____

_____

_____

_____

21

READING PURPOSEFULLY

TODAY'S PASSAGE:
Jeremiah 38

———

TIME COMMITMENT:
45 minutes

Purposeful reading looks for the aim of the author. There isn't a verse of Scripture that was thrown in by accident. Every word contributes to meaning. Your challenge as a reader is to discern that meaning" (p. 115).

At first reading, Jeremiah 38 tells an interesting story. But a purposeful examination of the chapter might reveal much more than a cursory reading. Read the chapter once to get your bearings. But then see how much additional information you can glean by using some of the suggestions for reading purposefully. (It may help to use some other Bible resources as needed.)

The passage is a bit long for a close examination of all the subjects and objects, modifiers, prepositional phrases, and such. But do any of the literary features stand out to you? (Present tense vs. future prophecies? Important connectives such as "but" or "and"? Etc.)

_____

_____

More than providing purpose through grammatical structure, this chapter lends itself to examination for purpose through literary structure. For example, this is a key event in the *biography* of Jeremiah. How does the passage fit into what you already know about the prophet?

_____

_____

From a *historical* basis, the story takes place during the rise of power of the Babylonian Empire. How is that important to the events taking place?

_____

_____

The *geography* of the account is the city of Jerusalem. In what ways is the location significant in this passage?

_____

_____

From an *ideological* perspective, suppose this chapter was all you knew about Jeremiah. What would you suppose might be the prophet's primary message?

_____

_____

As you read other chapters of Jeremiah at some point in the future, see if they confirm your presumptions or provide new information that causes you to change your mind.

It should be noted that in Jeremiah and certain other books of prophecy, the authors don't follow a strict chronological time line. If one event is described before another one, we can't necessarily assume that it took place first. We must use other of our purposeful methods to maintain a proper sense of order.

22

READING PURPOSEFULLY

TODAY'S PASSAGE:
Colossians 1:15–29

TIME COMMITMENT:
45 minutes

Two of the most powerful words in the Bible are *and* and *but*. . . . Another important connective is *therefore*. Whenever you see a *therefore*, go back and see what it's there for" (p. 117).

While the previous assignment in Jeremiah was a good study in purposeful reading via history, biography, geography, and so forth, now we turn our attention to a passage that will better allow us to examine grammar to understand the author's purpose.

Read Colossians 1:15–29 and answer the following questions.

- You won't find any *therefores* in this section (at least, not in the *New American Standard Bible*), but what other connectives can you find that help determine the purpose of what Paul was writing?

- Did you notice a change of verb tenses back and forth from past to present? What significant events have taken place in the past? How does what has been done in the past affect the present?

- One clear focus is on the person of Jesus Christ. Read the passage and record all the significant information you can gather about Jesus.

• A secondary focus is on the writer of the letter. What things does this section say about Paul?

_____

_____

• And don't miss the third focus on the benefits of the recipients of the letter. The Colossian church received a number of instructions and promises in this passage—and so do you and I. How many can you find?

_____

_____

• Finally, there's an important two-letter word in verse 23: *if.* It would have been simple enough for Paul to have omitted this clause. So what do you think was his purpose in adding it?

_____

_____

23

READING ACQUISITIVELY

TODAY'S PASSAGE:
You decide

TIME COMMITMENT:
Also up to you

Read the Bible acquisitively. That is, read not only to receive it but to retain it; not merely to perceive it but to possess it. Stake a claim on the text. Make it your own property" (p. 123).

For this assignment, you have a great degree of freedom to decide what to read and how to study it. Select any passage of Scripture you wish and read it acquisitively. In fact, pretend you're responsible for reporting on it in a creative way, and outline your presentation below. Here are some ideas for how to make your chosen passage come alive for someone else:

- Create a skit from the passage.
- Describe how to act out the passage (using puppets, mime, traditional drama, or whatever you think will work best).
- Rewrite the text. It might become a children's story, a news broadcast, a letter to a friend, a reading for a special occasion, etc.
- Investigate the passage like a detective. Check out all cross-references to the people and places mentioned, define any unfamiliar names or terms, etc.
- Design a banner with symbols and/or words to communicate the essence of the teaching in that section of the Bible.
- Anything goes. Come up with your own idea(s) for an effective presentation.

If you wish to follow the pattern of Bible reading we've established so far, you might want to select one passage from the Old Testament to read acquisitively, and then a second one from the New Testament. If you're doing these Bible studies with a partner or group, this is an excellent opportunity for you to work together.

What difference does it make whether you've read every page, and maybe even underlined parts of the text, if in the end you leave your Bible on the shelf and never get into it for yourself? My goal—and I hope yours as well—is to see life-change as a result of your personal interaction with God's Word" (pp. 124–25).

24

READING
TELESCOPICALLY

TODAY'S PASSAGE:
Lamentations 3:22–33

TIME COMMITMENT:
45 minutes

Whenever you come to a book of the Bible ask, Where does this book fit historically? When was it written? When did the events take place? What was happening elsewhere in the world at that time?" (p. 129)

Many people are fond of citing portions of today's assigned passage. It speaks of God's great love and faithfulness, and His compassions that never fail. What a positive and optimistic outlook, right?

We would venture to guess that only a small percentage of people who quote these verses have put them in context. Our assignment today is to take a telescopic approach to this passage. If you step back and examine the passage in its context, you'll find that it sits right in the middle of the book of Lamentations, a series of funeral dirges.

First read Lamentations 3:22–33—the portion that so many people telescope into. How do these verses make you feel about God?

_____

_____

_____

_____

The book of Lamentations isn't very long. Read it straight through in order to put the previous verses into their context. As you read these five chapters, make a list of events that are taking place during this time. (If you don't find war, cannibalism, and worse, you're not looking hard enough.) You might also want to consult a commentary to get more of a historical perspective on the conflicts described in Lamentations.

_____

_____

Reread Lamentations 3:22–33. Does the significance of this passage change from your previous reading? In what ways?

_____

_____

_____

25

READING TELESCOPICALLY

TODAY'S PASSAGE:
Hebrews 12:1–13

TIME COMMITMENT:
45 minutes

What happens in a lot of Bible study and Bible teaching is that we keep breaking it down and breaking it down, until we have nothing but baskets of fragments. What we need today are people who can put the parts back together again into a meaningful and powerful whole. So every time you read and analyze Scripture, every time you take it apart, realize that you've only done half the job. Your next task is to put it back together again" (pp. 127–28).

The author of Hebrews wanted to encourage us to endure hardships and be more disciplined. Read Hebrews 12:1–13 and summarize in a single sentence what you think he was trying to say.

_____

_____

We hope you noticed that the assigned passage had a couple of *therefores* in it—one at the very beginning and one near the end. They are clues that the telescope of Scripture is quite close. In order to back it up a bit and get our bearings, first review chapter 11 of Hebrews.

- How far back did the author go to set up what he was saying in chapter 12?

_____

_____

- What does Hebrews 11 have to add to what the author said about discipline in chapter 12?

_____

_____

The *therefore* in Hebrews 12:1 seems to be a link between the sufferings of people in the past with those of us in the present. After exhorting us to "endure hardship as discipline" (v. 7 NIV), what does the *therefore* in verse 12 connect to? To find out, read the rest of Hebrews 12 where you'll get to a third *therefore* (v. 28). The author is leading us from the heroic characters of the past . . . to our current sufferings . . . to what?

_____

_____

_____

Each of these sections of Hebrews is helpful on its own merit. But by reading telescopically and linking them together, we discover that their relationship to one another can be just as significant as their individual teachings.

26

WORKING WITH A PARAGRAPH

TODAY'S PASSAGE:
Jonah 4:5–8

TIME COMMITMENT:
30–60 minutes

The paragraph is the basic unit of study—not the verse, not the chapter. . . . The paragraph represents a complete thought. It is a group of related sentences and statements that deal with one main topic or idea. That makes it ideal for observational study" (p. 131).

By this time you've had ample opportunity to practice examining a single verse and applying various observational techniques to numerous passages of Scripture—long and short. Now we turn our attention to a single paragraph. The one we've selected from the Old Testament is Jonah 4:5–8. We've provided the *New American Standard Bible* version of this paragraph below, with plenty of space for you to take notes and make observations.

Then Jonah went out from the city and sat east of it. There he made a shelter for himself and sat under it in the shade until he could see what would happen in the city. So the Lord God appointed a plant and it grew up over Jonah to be a shade over his head to deliver him from his discomfort. And Jonah was extremely happy about the plant. But God appointed a worm when dawn came the next day and it attacked the plant and it withered. When the sun came up God appointed a scorching east wind, and the sun beat down on Jonah's head so that he became faint and begged with all his soul to die, saying, "Death is better to me than life."

This story is less familiar than Jonah's encounter with the great fish. But what you already know about Jonah should provide insight into this paragraph. Consider some of the following observations, and add others of your own.

- What is the "city" referred to?

_____

- Why is Jonah observing the city from a distance rather than residing in it?

_____

- Where does this story come chronologically in regard to Jonah's big fish experience?

_____

This paragraph is a study in contrasts. Consider the potential significance of the following ones, and then add others you find. What is noteworthy about:

- Jonah's expectation for the city versus God's?

_____

- Jonah's shelter versus God's shelter for Jonah?

_____

- Jonah's response to God's worm versus his previous response to God's fish?

_____

- God's gift of shade to Jonah versus His removal of that shade?

_____

- Jonah's attitude when comfortable versus his mind-set under adverse conditions?

_____

Jonah 1:17 tells us that "the Lord appointed [or provided] a great fish" just when Jonah was at risk of drowning. What three other things are "appointed" by God as described in this paragraph? What was the result of each one? What does this paragraph suggest about God's provisions for our lives?

_____

_____

What other observations do you make from this paragraph?

_____

_____

27

WORKING WITH A PARAGRAPH

TODAY'S PASSAGE:
2 Corinthians 4:7–12

TIME COMMITMENT:
30–60 minutes

How to work with a paragraph: (1) Check the context; (2) Label your observations; and (3) [Keep in mind that] no detail is trivial (pp. 131–37, from the section headings).

Below is a New Testament paragraph for you to observe and comment on. As before, we have provided the text and some questions to get you started.

But we have this treasure in earthen vessels, so that the surpassing greatness of the power will be of God and not from ourselves; we are afflicted in every way, but not crushed; perplexed, but not despairing; persecuted, but not forsaken; struck down, but not destroyed; always carrying about in the body the dying of Jesus, so that the life of Jesus also may be manifested in our body. For we who live are constantly being delivered over to death for Jesus' sake, so that the life of Jesus also may be manifested in our mortal flesh. So death works in us, but life in you.

A lot of themes go by quickly in this single paragraph: suffering, life, and death among others. It might help to know the author and whether or not he was truly an authority on what he was writing.

LIVING BY THE BOOK

Who wrote this passage?

_____

What is the "treasure" he referred to in the first sentence?

_____

What's the significance of "earthen vessels" (some translations read "jars of clay")? Isn't it foolish to keep "treasure" in such fragile containers?

_____

_____

What did the author know about suffering? Can you recall any instances where he was:

- afflicted? _____
- perplexed? _____
- persecuted? _____
- struck down? _____

(You may want to consult other passages or resources for specific examples.)

How about you? Can you relate to the conditions being described here? In what ways?

_____

_____

In what ways do we "carry about in the body the dying of Jesus"?

_____

_____

In what ways is the life of Jesus revealed in our bodies?

_____

_____

How can "death work[ing] in us" be connected to "life [working] in you"?

_____

_____

What other observations or questions come to mind in regard to this paragraph?

_____

_____

28

LOOKING FOR THINGS THAT ARE EMPHASIZED

TODAY'S PASSAGE:
Proverbs 31:10–31

TIME COMMITMENT:
30 minutes

The Bible uses several ways to emphasize material. Let me mention four: (1) Amount of space; (2) Stated purpose; (3) Order; and (4) Movement from the lesser to the greater, and vice versa" (pp. 143–46, from section headings).

A complaint some seekers and skeptics have about Scripture is what they perceive to be its lack of respect for women. Some people take issue with the male pronouns for God, the vast amount of material devoted to the patriarchs and other "guy stuff," and the instructions on submission in marriage. We like to think that Scripture certainly speaks more highly of women than the general cultures during which it was written. We also recognize the significance of the passages that highlight the value of women amid all the male stories. But when we come across a passage like Proverbs 31, the emphasis is significant indeed.

Read Proverbs 31:10–31. How would you feel if this were a speech delivered about you at a testimonial dinner?

_____

_____

_____

Since much of the book of Proverbs consists of bite-sized bits of wisdom, how does this passage emphasize its content based on the amount of space it gets?

_____

_____

_____

Does this passage have a stated purpose?

_____

_____

_____

Does its order in connection with the other material in Proverbs seem to emphasize or de-emphasize it? Why?

_____

_____

_____

Do you detect any other ways in which the author emphasizes that this is an important passage?

_____

_____

_____

What qualities are emphasized in this passage?

_____

_____

_____

Let's hear it for this very important emphasis that draws our attention to and requires our admiration of women of noble character everywhere!

29

LOOKING FOR THINGS THAT ARE EMPHASIZED

TODAY'S PASSAGE:
Luke 15

TIME COMMITMENT:
20 minutes

The first clue to look for when you come to the Scriptures is that which is emphasized. The writers have gone to great trouble to hang out a sign that says, 'Hey, this is important. Pay attention' " (p. 147).

The account of the Prodigal Son is a beloved parable that speaks to the heart. But have you even noticed how it seems to be emphasized in Scripture?

If you begin reading Luke 15, first you find the story of a lost sheep (vv. 1–7). What percentage of the flock was lost?

_____

What do you suppose would be the value of a single sheep in that society?

_____

_____

As you continue reading, you come across the story of a lost coin (vv. 8–10). What percentage of coins was lost?

_____

What was the value of the lost coin? (Consult some other references.)

_____

_____

Jesus, the master storyteller, moves from the tale of a lost sheep, to the story of a lost coin, to the parable of the prodigal son. Read Luke 15:11–32. The amount of space devoted to this final story immediately gives it greater emphasis. The order of the stories also seems to "save the best for last."

What percentage of the father's sons was lost?

_____

What was the value of the lost son to the father?

_____

_____

The impact of the parable of the prodigal son is powerful, even as a "stand alone" story. But it becomes even more poignant as the result of moving from the lesser to the greater. In its context within Luke 15, do you see how Jesus placed extra emphasis on it? Why do you think He did so?

_____

_____

_____

30

LOOKING FOR THINGS
THAT ARE REPEATED

> **TODAY'S PASSAGE:**
> *Joshua 1*
>
> ———
>
> **TIME COMMITMENT:**
> *30 minutes*

There's probably no tool of teaching more powerful than repetition. If I want to make sure that you catch on to what I have to say, I'll repeat it over and over, again and again, time after time. Repetition reinforces" (p. 148).

Suppose you've been chosen to replace a beloved leader who has served faithfully for decades. You're a good person, but you've got some big shoes to fill. Your own record is a little sparse, and you might have a few doubts about yourself: Will the people accept me? Can I take over a huge responsibility without wrecking the organization? Will I become as popular as my predecessor?

Would you have any other concerns?

_____

_____

What kinds of affirmation would you desire if you found yourself in this situation?

_____

_____

Read Joshua 1. This passage records what God told Joshua as the younger leader was being called to replace Moses. Ahead of him lies Jericho and numerous other fortified cities that he must get through to possess the Promised Land. Many of us would be shaking in our sandals.

What phrase can you find that is repeated in this chapter?

_____

_____

Why do you think such repetition was used?

_____

_____

From whom did Joshua hear this phrase? (You should find two answers.)

_____

_____

Can you find a repeated emphasis on anything else in this passage?

_____

_____

Perhaps you've heard the phrase: "God said it. I believe it. That settles it." Well, in some cases God says something and then repeats it. Whenever we find such repetition in Scripture, the issue is never settled until we see, believe, and *respond* to it.

31
LOOKING FOR THINGS THAT ARE REPEATED

TODAY'S PASSAGE:
Romans 7:7–25

TIME COMMITMENT:
30 minutes

In short, whenever you study the Bible and notice that something is repeated—said more than once—mark it down. It's not because the writers couldn't think of anything else to say. It's their way of pointing out matters of crucial importance" (p. 151).

This assignment may be a bit more challenging than the previous one. Read through Romans 7:7–25 a few times and see if you can find what is repeated most frequently. If you need help, a couple of clues are provided at the end of this chapter.

Do you think it is unusual for an author to repeat himself in this manner? Why or why not?

_____

_____

_____

Before long we're going to get into some exercises where we're looking for things that are alike or unlike. As a preview, what examples can you find in this passage?

_____

_____

_____

What would you say is the theme of this passage?

_____

_____

_____

As Paul moved from this theme to the topic of a life controlled by the Holy Spirit (Romans 8), his very perspective and writing style changed. Count all the first person singular pronouns (I, me, mine, myself, etc.) in the Romans 7 passage. Then compare that number with all you find in Romans 8. The good news of Romans 8 is highlighted as Paul moved from speaking so frequently about himself (I . . . I . . . I) into what the Spirit of God makes possible for all believers. The heavy use of repetition, followed by an abrupt end to such repetition, seems to give more impact to what he was saying.

HINT The repeated word is very short. In fact, it's only one letter. It's also a first person singular pronoun that can be found in the following words: HI, IT, IS, and PI.

32

LOOKING FOR THINGS THAT ARE RELATED

TODAY'S PASSAGE:
Numbers 21:4–9

———

TIME COMMITMENT:
30 minutes

By 'related' I mean things that have some connection, some interaction with each other. You see, just because two things are next to each other does not make them related. They've got to work off of each other in some way. There must be a tie that somehow binds them together" (p. 153).

Various components of Scripture can be related through (1) movement from the general to the specific; (2) questions and answers; or (3) cause and effect. Today's assignment focuses on the third category.

Read Numbers 21:4–9. List all the things you see where one action (the cause) led directly to another (the effect).

_____

_____

_____

_____

The examples in this account are fairly obvious. They shouldn't be hard to discover. But let's now consider that Jesus used this story as an illustration of His own mission in life. Read John 3:14–15. What cause and effect pattern was Jesus referring to?

_____

_____

Do you think Jesus just happened to use this story as an allegory for His own plans? Or do you think perhaps the solution to the Israelites' sin in the wilderness was a prediction of what was to come?

_____

If you chose the latter response to the previous question, would you consider this a case of a related event, moving from a general to a specific event? Why or why not?

33

LOOKING FOR THINGS
THAT ARE RELATED

TODAY'S PASSAGE:
John 3:1–21

———

TIME COMMITMENT:
20 minutes

The question is one of the most powerful tools of communication. If I ask you a question, doesn't it more or less force you to think? Sure it does. Of course, if someone only asks questions and never provides answers, that can be very frustrating. You begin to wonder whether he knows what he's talking about. But we're going to discover that the biblical writers employ both—strategic questions and helpful answers" (p. 155).

Several examples of potent questions and answers were provided in the original *Living by the Book* text (p. 155). But for this exercise, we want to look at a question that wasn't particularly good. In fact, it was quite ridiculous.

Read John 3:1–9. You'll probably recognize the story. It's where Nicodemus and Jesus were having a late-night conversation. Jesus was trying to pass along some deep insight about spiritual things, but Nicodemus wasn't exactly soaking it up like a sponge. What "deep" questions did he have for Jesus?

_____

_____

_____

Now read John 3:10–21. What were some of the other things Jesus had to tell Nicodemus?

_____

_____

_____

Among the things you noted should have been the classic verse: John 3:16. We all love this verse! But look at the circumstances under which Jesus uttered it. It was in response to a question—a rather simplistic question, but a question nevertheless. What if Nicodemus had been reluctant to sound foolish and had never asked Jesus to explain Himself further? Do you think we would be quoting John 3:16 today?

_____

_____

Jesus' response to Nicodemus's question is only one of many examples of the question-and-answer format of things that are related in Scripture. What do you think it suggests to us about asking "stupid" questions if we don't understand something in Scripture?

_____

_____

_____

34
LOOKING FOR THINGS THAT ARE ALIKE

> **TODAY'S PASSAGE:**
> *Isaiah 66:1–16*
>
> **TIME COMMITMENT:**
> *40 minutes*

The biblical writers give you a number of terms that flag similarities. The two most common words to look for are *as* and *like*. They indicate a figure of speech called a 'simile,' which is a word picture that draws a comparison between two things. . . . A device related to the simile is the metaphor, where comparison is made without using *as* or *like*" (pp. 158–59).

We hope the introduction of similes and metaphors doesn't trigger any unpleasant flashbacks to freshman English class. But quite simply, they are too important to ignore when it comes to observing Scripture. In cases like today's assignment, they are used to help people understand a God who is indescribable. By using things that *can* be described, we are drawn into a closer understanding of what God is like.

This passage is somewhat challenging. God's message contains much that is unpleasant, because His people had been unfaithful. Yet beneath the severe tone is always an affirmation that, indeed, God loves His people. The better we come to see God's anger directed at sin, the more we can comprehend His unconditional love toward the sinner.

First read Isaiah 66:1–16 as an English student. As you go through it, list all the metaphors and similes you find. When you finish, read the same passage again, this time as a Bible student. Use your list of metaphors and similes, and this time put some thought into what each comparison tells you about God.

Take your time, because this passage contains several good examples. Read slowly and carefully. Work your way through the difficult sections and see what conclusions you can come to about what God is saying.

SIMILES OR METAPHORS
Heaven is My throne (v. 1)

WHAT THE COMPARISON MEANS
The magnitude of God's authority is unlimited

35

LOOKING FOR THINGS
THAT ARE ALIKE

TODAY'S PASSAGE:
Matthew 23:23–39

TIME COMMITMENT:
30 minutes

Keep in mind that similarities have a way of drawing attention to themselves. Nevertheless, get into the habit of looking for them. You'll find them especially in the wisdom literature, particularly in the psalms. Whenever you find one, mark it. The writer is trying to communicate with you through the effective tool of comparison" (pp. 160–61).

Today's assignment is a bit similar to the previous one. (After all, we're focusing on things that are alike.) This time we're looking at a discourse by Jesus concerning the hypocrisy of the Pharisees. Read Matthew 23:23–39. Record each place where Jesus compares one thing to another and determine what you think is Jesus' point in each case.

JESUS' COMPARISONS

WHAT THE COMPARISON MEANS

36

LOOKING FOR THINGS
THAT ARE UNLIKE

TODAY'S PASSAGE:
Numbers 13:25–14:31

TIME COMMITMENT:
30 minutes

The flip side of comparison is contrast—things that are unlike. We could say that in Bible study, as in love, opposites attract. At least, they attract the eye of the observant reader. There are several ways the biblical writers signify contrast. . . . The word *but* is a clue that a change of direction is coming" (p. 161).

Today's assignment is a passage that occurs just as the twelve spies return from scouting out the Promised Land. The nation of Israel has come out of the slavery of Egypt, through the Red Sea, and across the desert. They are poised at the brim of the land to which God has led them. They've faced a lot of challenges and done a lot of grumbling, but all they need is a report from their advance men, and they can complete their journey.

Read Numbers 13:25–14:10. If you look carefully, you'll notice that almost every time a positive theme begins to develop, you'll find a word such as *but* or *nevertheless* followed by a section quite unlike what had preceded it. Where are the turning points in this passage? (You should find at least three.)

_____

_____

_____

Then, in an ironic twist, God begins to speak to Moses and pass judgment on the people. His sentence is a hard one, clear about the suffering and death that will take place during the next forty years. And in this section, almost every place you find the word *but* it is to make a positive exception. Read Numbers 14:11–31. Look for the *buts* and an occasional *except,* and note whom God singles out as being unlike the rest of the unfaithful Israelites.

_____

_____

When you start noticing the negative connective words, it's amazing to discover how quickly the tone of the passage can change. It's a simple matter to detect things that are unlike in the passage, which may then lead to more in-depth discoveries of what Scripture is saying.

37

LOOKING FOR THINGS THAT ARE UNLIKE

TODAY'S PASSAGE:
Acts 4:32–5:11

———

TIME COMMITMENT:
20 minutes

Things that are alike and unlike make use of the strong human tendency to compare and contrast. As you study the Scriptures, listen to that voice inside your head saying, 'Hey, this is like that passage I looked at yesterday,' or, 'This section is different from anything else in this book.' Those are clear signals that the author is using things alike and unlike to communicate his message" (p. 163).

If you begin to read through Acts about the formation of the new church, you come upon a passage about a couple very much unlike the rest of the people described.

Read Acts 4:32–37, which describes the "alike" people of the early church. Suppose you were a first-century visitor who happened to drop in for a worship service. How do you think you would have responded? Why?

_____

_____

Now read Acts 5:1–11. The introduction of Ananias and Sapphira brings an abrupt shift in the tone of the passage. Why were they so unlike the people previously described?

_____

_____

Suppose you were a first-century visitor to the church on the day the events of Acts 5 took place. How do you think you would have responded? Why?

_____

_____

The use of irony is another thing to watch for in determining the importance of things alike or unlike. Do you detect any irony in this passage, especially in regard to the deaths of Ananias and Sapphira?

_____

_____

_____

As we examine this clear biblical example of something unlike something else, what do you think is the message for us?

_____

_____

_____

38

LOOKING FOR THINGS THAT ARE TRUE TO LIFE

TODAY'S PASSAGE:
1 Kings 11

TIME COMMITMENT:
30 minutes

Often we study or teach Scripture as if it were some academic lesson, rather than real life. No wonder so many of us are bored with our Bibles. We're missing out on the best lessons of God's Word by failing to pick up on the experiences of the people in it. . . . What I love about the Bible is that it always returns me to reality. It never paints its characters with whitewash. If necessary, it hangs the dirty laundry right out the front window to tell me what really happened" (pp. 165–66).

Are you the kind of person who frequently ponders, "If only . . ."?

"If only I had more money, I could spend more time for God." "If only I were a bit smarter, I could have a better job." "If only I could move up in the world, I could make more of a difference on those around me."

Sometimes we focus our attention on the success stories of the Bible and feel very inferior spiritually as well as emotionally. But it's always a mistake to compare our own failures with someone else's successes. Let's instead check our failures against theirs. And perhaps there's no better example to examine than King Solomon.

Before you read today's passage, skim through 1 Kings 3:20–4:34 and 10:14–29 (as well as any other stories about Solomon's reign you might want to review). At this time, Solomon was perhaps the richest man on earth. He was certainly the wisest. His kingdom was at peace. Spiritually, he was the one who had built and dedicated the Lord's temple. He never had to wonder what life would be like "if only." He could see for himself.

We can read about most of the events of his reign and wonder what's there for us, something that *we* might find to be "true to life." Then we come to 1 Kings 11—literally the final "chapter" in Solomon's life.

Read 1 Kings 11:1–13. Consider:

- How could someone as wise as Solomon make the mistake he did?

_____

_____

- Why do you think Solomon got involved with *so many* women?

_____

_____

- What did Solomon's human relationships have to do with his relationship with God?

_____

_____

- What lessons can you find in this section that are just as true to life today as they were in Solomon's time? In addition to obvious observations (improper physical relationships, spiritual apostasy, etc.), look for other lessons as well. For example, Solomon didn't receive the full brunt of God's displeasure. Is that something you can relate to? Or perhaps you can understand what it's like to have a future that doesn't look as bright as you might hope, yet isn't exactly hopeless.

_____

_____

_____

If you look closely, you're likely to find more things that are true to your life than you anticipated.

39

LOOKING FOR THINGS THAT ARE TRUE TO LIFE

TODAY'S PASSAGE:
2 Timothy 1

———

TIME COMMITMENT:
30 minutes

There's a ring of authenticity to the accounts of [Bible characters]. But it's easy to miss if your eyes are not looking for things that are true to life. When you study the Word of God, make sure you plug it into real life. Then you will discover that the people in the biblical narrative are just like you and me. They are cut out of the same bolt of human cloth" (p. 168).

In the last chapter we looked at Solomon, a man who had wealth, power, title, wisdom, prestige, and God's endorsement as king. Yet in spite of everything he had going for him, he lost faith late in life and suffered the consequences.

Today we look at an opposite extreme—Timothy. A young man called to the ministry, Timothy had several strikes against him. His mother and grandmother were believers in Jesus, but apparently his father wasn't (Acts 16:1). In addition, Timothy was young and probably somewhat shy. It's not exactly a profile that many business consultants would choose to pair with the bold apostle Paul. But God saw the potential in Timothy, and Paul became a mentor for the young pastor.

Read 2 Timothy 1. As you do, note anything that rings true to life, based on your own experiences. For example:

- Do you know mothers or grandmothers who go out of their way to see that their children grow up properly, including an exposure to spiritual things?

- Do you know someone who is a strong Christian, even though his or her home life wasn't exactly ideal?

_____

_____

- Do you know of any "odd pairings" when it comes to one person working to disciple another? What have been the results of such relationships?

_____

_____

- Who has been a "Paul" in your own life?

_____

_____

- Who has been a "Timothy"?

_____

_____

Paul offered Timothy praise, encouragement, challenges, sharing of deep personal feelings, and more. List the people you would consider your "children" (whether literally or in a spiritual sense). What are you doing for each person to care for his or her emotional and spiritual life? What else would you like to do for the people who come to your mind?

_____

_____

_____

_____

What other true-to-life observations can you make from this passage of Scripture?

_____

_____

_____

40
WORKING WITH A SEGMENT OF SCRIPTURE

TODAY'S PASSAGE:
Field trip

TIME COMMITMENT:
1–2 hours

A chart . . . is invaluable, because it gives you a maximum return on your investment in the Bible study process. Every time you come back to this passage, you can pull out your chart and quickly review what the section is all about. You don't have to start from scratch every time. Neither do you have to rely on your memory" (p. 178).

The next couple of assignments are going to ask you to design your own charts for lengthy sections of Scripture. Before doing so, you might want to take a day for review and research. We suggest you do at least two things to prepare.

(1) Review chapters 24 and 25 in *Living by the Book*. A variety of hints and examples are provided for you there, which should help you start thinking in creative ways. (Several of the key suggestions are reprinted in the next two chapters of this workbook.)

(2) Take a "field trip" to a library or bookstore. Spend some time in the biblical reference section, flipping through books to see how many kinds of charts you can find. Some will be rather simple; others will be quite complex. See how various scholars condense and present large amounts of information into an easy-to-read chart.

Don't go looking for the "right" way to make a chart. Many people might examine the same passage of Scripture and come up with a completely different—yet equally effective—way to present the material. Instead, look more for variety. Then when you begin to think of how to compose your own charts, you'll have a good assortment of possibilities to get you started.

41
HOW TO STUDY A
SECTION OF SCRIPTURE

(1) Read the entire section completely. In fact, try reading it two or three times, perhaps in different translations.

(2) Identify the paragraphs, and put a label or title on each paragraph. Remember that the paragraph is the basic unit of study. So it's important to grasp the main idea or theme of each paragraph, and then state that in a word or two.

(3) Evaluate each paragraph in light of the other paragraphs. Use the six clues you've already learned: things that are emphasized, things that are repeated, things that are related, things that are alike, things that are unlike, and things that are true to life.

(4) Evaluate how the section as a whole relates to the rest of the book, using the same six principles.

(5) Try to state the main point of the section. See if you can boil it down to one word or a short phrase that summarizes the content.

(6) Keep a list of observations on the section. Better yet, record them in your Bible, using brief, descriptive words.

(7) Study the persons and places mentioned. See what you can learn about them that throws light on the section as a whole.

(8) Keep a list of your unanswered questions and unresolved problems. Those become avenues for further investigation.

(9) Ask yourself: What have I seen in this section that challenges the way I live? What practical issues does this passage address? What change do I need to consider in light of this study? What prayer do I need to pray as a result of what I've seen?

(10) Share the results of your study with someone else.

These suggestions are reprinted from the end of chapter 24 of *Living by the Book*. If you desire further review, you'll find more specific examples in that chapter.

42

MAKING A START WITH YOUR CHART

(1) As you study a text, assign titles and labels to the content in a way that summarizes the material. Be creative. Placing your own titles on the verses, paragraphs, sections, and books of the Bible is one way to "read acquisitively" and make the text your own. They help you retain your insights in neat packages.

(2) As you visualize your chart, ask: What are the relationships? What am I trying to show? What's this chart all about? When I've finished it, how am I going to use it?

(3) Keep your charts simple. You can always add detail; the challenge is to trim away the clutter. What key ideas, characters, themes, verses, terms, and other data from the text ought to take priority? What is the big idea? What structure needs to be shown? What material do you want to see at a glance?

(4) If you find that you've got too much material to include in a chart, chop it up and make several charts. By the way, too much unrelated data is a clue that you need to go back to the text and do some more observing.

(5) Be creative. There are dozens of ways to show relationships in the text. Let your imagination flow. Draw illustrations or symbols if they help. It's your chart, so make it work for you.

(6) Revise your charts in light of your study. No chart can summarize everything. As you continue to study a passage, you'll gain new insights that should cause you to revise or even redo your chart. Remember, charts are a means to an end, not an end in themselves. They are useful to the extent that they accurately represent what is in the biblical text.

These steps are reprinted from the end of chapter 25 of *Living by the Book*. If you desire further review, you'll find more specific examples in that chapter.

43

WORKING WITH A SEGMENT OF SCRIPTURE

TODAY'S PASSAGE:
Exodus 7–12

TIME COMMITMENT:
60 minutes

Bible study is information-intensive. If you do the job of observation [as previously described], you'll have more data than you can possibly handle. And that's a problem, because what good is information if you can't access it? . . . Show rather than tell. Summarize your findings in a chart" (p. 181).

Lots of people can tell you that Moses called down several plagues on the Egyptians before Pharaoh would let the Israelites leave. Some people even know there were ten such plagues. But few people are able to quickly list all ten.

Today's assignment is to create a chart that will help you identify the plagues as well as take note of anything else you feel is relevant about them. (The immediate effects of each one? The reactions of the Egyptians and/or Israelites? The response of Pharaoh to each one? Etc.)

The account of the plagues is found in Exodus 7:14–12:42. Your task is to figure how to summarize the key information in that section of Scripture by means of a chart. Use the hints on the previous sheets, and don't hurry into the project until you have an idea in mind.

Don't feel bad if you need to start over several times. Finding the right outline to follow is the hardest part. But once you get past that point, all that's left is the rather simple matter of filling in the blanks.

44

WORKING WITH A SEGMENT OF SCRIPTURE

TODAY'S PASSAGE:
Revelation 2–3

TIME COMMITMENT:
60 minutes

A chart is to the Bible student what a map is to a mariner. It aids him or her in navigating an ocean of words, pages, books, ideas, characters, events, and other information. Without a chart or some similar device, he is liable to founder on the shoals of mental overload. There are just too many details to keep track of" (p. 181).

In the first part of the book of Revelation we are told of an awe-inspiring vision of Jesus, who dictated a series of letters to seven different churches. John did a lot of writing to pass along the message verbatim. However, the letters all follow a clear pattern. Read Revelation 2–3 several times until you get a feel for the structure of the letters. Then create a chart that can help you visualize all that information more simply.

When you finish, you should be able to use your chart in a number of different ways. By going one way (either left to right or up and down), you will have a concise analysis of the spiritual condition of each of the seven churches. But if you look at the chart the other way, you will have assembled a comparison of how various churches were performing in a number of different categories.

Again, make this chart your own. It's more important to create something that is meaningful to you instead of something fancy or complex.

Part 2

INTERPRETATION

FROM OBSERVATION TO INTERPRETATION

As we make a transition from Observation to Interpretation, let's review a few key points from the *Living by the Book* text. The next several pages provide some essential reminders about the importance of Interpretation, some hazards to avoid, and the various types of biblical literature you might come across in your attempts to interpret Scripture.

45

WHY DO WE NEED INTERPRETATION?

Why must we interpret Scripture? Why can't we just open the Word, read what we're supposed to do, and then do it? Why do we have to go to so much trouble to understand the text? The answer is that time and distance have thrown up barriers between us and the biblical writers, which block our understanding. We need to appreciate what those roadblocks are. They are not insurmountable, but they are substantial (p. 198).

LANGUAGE BARRIERS

Have you ever learned a foreign language? If so, you know that learning the words is not enough. You have to learn the mind-set, the culture, the worldview of those who speak it if you really want to understand what they are saying.

In the same way, when it comes to the Bible, we have some excellent translations from the Hebrew, Greek, and Aramaic languages in which it was originally written. Even so, the English text leaves us a long way from a complete understanding. That's why the process of Interpretation involves the use of a Bible dictionary and similar resources. We have to go back and recover the shades of meaning that translated words alone cannot convey.

CULTURAL BARRIERS

These are closely related to the problems of language because language is always culture bound. The Bible is the product and presentation of cultures that are dramatically different from our own—and also different from each other. To appreciate what is going on in Scripture, we have to reconstruct the cultural context in areas of communication, transportation, trade, agriculture, occupations, religion, perceptions of time, and so on. Archaeology proves helpful in this area.

LITERARY BARRIERS

Another problem we run into in interpreting Scripture is the variety of the terrain. If it were all mountains or desert or ocean, we could outfit ourselves appropriately and have at it. But the literary genres of the Bible are quite diverse and demand vastly different approaches. We can't read the Song of Songs with the same cold logic that we bring to Romans. We won't get the point of the parables through the same exhaustive word studies that might unlock truths in Galatians.

COMMUNICATION BARRIERS

Even though God Himself was working to communicate through the writers of Scripture, we still must contend with breakdowns in the communication process. As finite creatures, we can never know what is going on in someone else's mind completely. As a result, we have to settle for limited objectives in our interpretation of Scripture.

46

AIDS TO INTERPRETATION

Have you ever felt shut out of understanding the Bible because you don't know the languages in which they were originally written? You don't have to feel that way any longer, thanks to the many extrabiblical resources that have been developed in recent years. . . . [Here are some resources] to help you interpret Scripture accurately (p. 201; also chart below).

TYPE OF RESOURCE	DESCRIPTION	USE IT TO OVERCOME . . .
Atlases	Collections of maps showing places mentioned in the text, and perhaps some description of their history and significance	Geographic barriers
Bible dictionaries	Explain the origin, meaning, and use of key words and terms in the text	Language barriers
Bible handbooks	Present helpful information on subjects in the text	Cultural barriers
Commentaries	Present a biblical scholar's study of the text	Language, cultural, and literary barriers
Interlinear texts	Translations with the Greek or Hebrew text positioned in between the lines for comparison	Language barriers

47

HAZARDS
TO AVOID

Here are six pitfalls of Interpretation to watch for as you study the Scriptures.

MISREADING THE TEXT

You'll never gain a proper understanding of Scripture if you don't or can't read the text properly. Ignorance of what the text says is the unpardonable sin of interpretation. It shows that you really haven't done your homework. You've skipped the first step in Bible study method—Observation.

DISTORTING THE TEXT

It's one thing to struggle with difficulties in interpretation; it's another thing to distort the meaning of God's Word. That's serious. That's something He will bring to judgment. So we need to be careful to learn how to interpret Scripture accurately, practically, and profitably.

CONTRADICTING THE TEXT

Contradicting the text is even worse than textual distortion. It amounts to calling God a liar. Satan has been lying from the beginning of history, and he's still lying today by encouraging people to contradict the biblical text. One of his favorite strategies is to use the words of God to authorize a belief or practice that goes against the character of God.

SUBJECTIVISM

Many Christians tolerate a form of mysticism in reading their Bibles that they would allow in no other realm. They violate every tenet of reason and common sense. Their Bible study is totally subjective. They wander around the Scriptures, waiting for a "liver-quiver" to tell them when they've struck pay dirt. There's nothing wrong with having an emotional reaction to the Word of God. But the meaning of the text is in the text, not in our subjective response to the text.

RELATIVISM

Some people approach Scripture assuming that the Bible changes meaning over time. They believe the text meant one thing when it was written but something else today; its meaning is relative. A passage can have numerous practical applications. But it can have only one proper interpretation, one meaning—ultimately, the meaning it had to the original writer. We must reconstruct his message if we want an accurate understanding.

OVERCONFIDENCE

In Bible study, as in life, pride goes before a fall. The minute you think that you've mastered a portion of Scripture, you are setting yourself up for a tumble. Some of the worst abuses of doctrine occur when someone sets himself up as the ultimate authority on the text. Keep in mind that Interpretation never ends. You can never come to the end of your study and say, "Well, I've got that one. I know that passage."

48
LITERARY GENRES
OF THE BIBLE

GENRE	CHARACTERISTICS	BIBLICAL BOOKS AND/OR EXAMPLES
Apocalyptic	Dramatic, highly symbolic material; vivid imagery stark contrasts; events take place on a global scale; frequently narrated in the firstperson as an eyewitness account; portrays a cosmic struggle between good and evil.	Revelation
Biography	Close-up view of an individual's life; the subject is often portrayed in contrast to someone else; selected events reveal character development, either positively (comedy) or negatively (tragedy).	Abraham, Isaac, Jacob, Joseph, Moses, Saul, David, Elijah, Jesus
Encomium	Sings high praise of someone or something; rehearses in glowing terms the subject's origins, acts, attributes, or superiority; exhorts the reader to incorporate the same features into his own life.	1 Samuel 2:1–10 Psalms 19; 119 Proverbs 8:22–36 Proverbs 31:10–31 Song of Songs John 1:1–18 1 Corinthians 13 Colossians 1:15–20 Hebrews 1–3
Exposition	Carefully reasoned argument or explanation; well-organized; logical flow; terms are crucial; builds to a logical, compelling climax; the aim is agreement and action.	Paul's letters Hebrews James 1 and 2 Peter 1, 2, and 3 John Jude
Narrative	A broad category in which story is prominent; includes historical accounts; structure is conveyed through plot; characters undergo psychological and spiritual development; selected events used to convey meaning; events juxtaposed for contrast and comparison.	Genesis–Ezra The Gospels Acts
Oratory	Stylized oral presentation of an argument; uses formal conventions of rhetoric and oratory; frequently quotes from authorities well-known to listeners; usually intended to exhort and persuade.	John 13–17 Acts 7 Acts 17:22–31 Acts 22:1–21 Acts 24:10–21 Acts 26:1–23

GENRE	CHARACTERISTICS	BIBLICAL BOOKS AND/OR EXAMPLES
Parable	Brief oral story illustrating a moral; truth frequently relies on stock characters and stereotypes; presents scenes and activities common to everyday life; encourages reflection and self-evaluation.	2 Samuel 12:1–6 Ecclesiastes 9:14–16 Matthew 13:1–53 Mark 4:1–34 Luke 15–16
Pastoral	Literature dealing with rural, rustic themes, especially shepherds; heavy on description, lean on action; often meditative and quiet; emphasis on the bond between a shepherd and his sheep; idealized presentation of life away from urban evils.	Psalm 23 Isaiah 40:11 John 10:1–18
Poetry	Verse intended to be spoken or sung rather than read; emphasis on cadence and the sounds of words; vivid images and symbols; appeals to the emotions; may employ features of encomium, pastoral, and other literary styles; in the Old Testament, heavy use of parallelism.	Job Psalms Proverbs Ecclesiastes Song of Songs
Prophecy	Strident, authoritative presentation of God's will and words; frequently intended as a corrective; intended to motivate change through warnings; foretells God's plans in response to human choices.	Isaiah–Malachi
Proverb	Short, pithy statement of a moral truth; reduces life to black-and-white categories; often addressed to youth; frequently employs parallelism; points readers toward the right and away from evil; heavy use of metaphors and similes.	Proverbs
Satire	Exposes and ridicules human vice and foolishness; is employed by various literary styles, especially narrative, biography, and proverb; warns readers through a negative example.	Proverbs 24:30–34 Ezekiel 34 Luke 18:1–8 2 Corinthians 11:1–12:1
Tragedy	Relates the downfall of a person; uses selected events to show the path toward ruin; problems usually revolve around a critical flaw in the person's character and moral choices; warns readers through a negative example.	Lot Samson King Saul Acts 5:1–11
Wisdom Literature	A broad category in which an older, seasoned person relates wisdom to a younger; may use parable; gives observations on fundamental areas of life—birth, death, work, money, power, time, the earth, and so on; appeals on the basis of human experience.	Job Proverbs Psalm 37 Psalm 90 Ecclesiastes

49

EXAMINING
THE CONTENT

TODAY'S PASSAGE:
Habakkuk 3:17–19

TIME COMMITMENT:
30 minutes

There is a direct cause-effect relationship between content and meaning. The content of a passage is the raw material, the database, with which you will interpret the text. And because of your work in Observation, you already know quite a bit about how to determine the content of a passage" (p. 223).

As we move from Observation to Interpretation, we'll start with a short passage to get some practice. For the next five days we'll look at Habakkuk 3:17–19 and practice various ways to interpret what's there. (Before long we will get to a couple of book studies where we plan to integrate all the elements of Bible study we've been learning, so we won't get too deep at this point.)

Read Habakkuk 3:17–19. Remember to look for terms, structure, literary form, and atmosphere. Try to find things that are emphasized, repeated, related, alike, unlike, or true to life. Then answer the following questions:

Who wrote this passage? To whom was he writing? (If you notice that the author did not address his people, you will have found something that makes this book unlike most other books of prophecy.)

_____

_____

_____

- What is happening? What point was the author trying to make?

_____

_____

_____

- Where was the author as he wrote this passage?

_____

_____

_____

- When (generally) was this written? (We'll look more closely at the context in the next assignment.)

_____

_____

- Why did the author portray such a bleak setting? Why did he feel the need to be so affirming in light of the scene he described?

_____

_____

_____

So what? As you look at this passage, what light can it shed on your life today? How can you take the things you've observed and begin to interpret them in a way that makes sense to you?

_____

_____

_____

_____

50
LOOKING FOR CONTEXT

TODAY'S PASSAGE:
Habakkuk 3:17–19

TIME COMMITMENT:
30 minutes

Context refers to that which goes before and that which follows after. . . . Whenever you study a verse, a paragraph, a section, even an entire book—always consult the neighbors of that verse, that paragraph, that section, that book. Whenever you get lost, climb a contextual tree and gain some perspective" (pp. 225, 227).

As we look again at the Habakkuk 3:17–19 passage, we want to move from content to context. Read these verses again. What's your first impression of Habakkuk's level of faith in God?

To begin to form a *literary context*, go back and read Habakkuk 3:16. How does that single verse influence the tone of the verses that follow?

_____

_____

_____

Now go back and read the Book of Habakkuk. (It's short.) What is the context of the closing passage in light of the rest of the book?

_____

_____

_____

_____

What is significant from a *historical context*? You should have already determined when the book was being written. But what else was going on in the world at that time? What is significant about Habakkuk's message from a political aspect?

_____

_____

_____

_____

_____

We'll save the *cultural context* until later (pp. 123–24). But from a *geographic context,* what might be changing for Habakkuk's people? In other words, what geographic relocation of people is likely to take place if the "nation invading us" (3:16 NIV) is successful?

_____

_____

_____

_____

_____

Finally, what can you determine about the *theological context* of this passage? What kind of relationship did Habakkuk seem to have with God? How does this passage compare with other prophetic passages you might be familiar with? What, ultimately, was God trying to communicate to Habakkuk? What was Habakkuk trying to communicate to God?

_____

_____

_____

_____

_____

51
MAKING RELEVANT COMPARISONS

TODAY'S PASSAGE:
Habakkuk 3:17–19

———

TIME COMMITMENT:
30 minutes

In comparison we compare Scripture with Scripture. And that offers a great safety net, because the greatest interpreter of Scripture is Scripture itself. . . . Comparison points out the great need you have for a concordance" (pp. 230–31).

Most of us cannot relate to living in a city being attacked by outsiders. While we may see news stories of locations where this kind of threat is still very real today, most of us are free of such fears. So how do we relate to what Habakkuk was saying here? Let's try to make a few comparisons.

Get a concordance and look for some comparative Scriptures. Naturally, you can spend all day perusing Scripture for comparisons. But take a few moments to do something that appeals to you. Here are a few suggestions, but feel free to create your own comparison study.

Can you find other examples of when a fig tree does not bud? What are the circumstances? What are the lessons to be learned?

_____

_____

_____

What else can you find about grapes and/or vines that might shed some light on this passage?

_____

_____

_____

Are there other places where *deer* ("hind") is used as a symbol of a person under God's care?

_____

_____

_____

Why do you think Habakkuk differentiated between "the Lord" (v. 18), "the God of my salvation" (v. 18), and "the Lord God" (v. 19)?

_____

_____

_____

52

CONSIDERING THE CULTURE

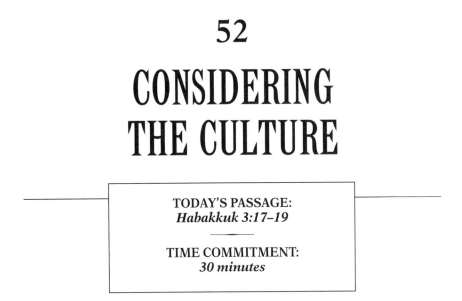

TODAY'S PASSAGE:
Habakkuk 3:17–19

TIME COMMITMENT:
30 minutes

When you study . . . any portion of the Word of God . . . make sure you study the background. Re-create the culture. Because then and only then will the text come alive" (p. 242).

It is possible that you grow grapes or olives for a living. Or you may just happen to be a shepherd. But if not, you'll need to put yourself in the place of a farmer many centuries ago as you again examine Habakkuk 3:17–19.

The passage describes someone waiting "fruitlessly" (if you'll excuse the pun) to see figs and olives bud out on trees and grapes spring forth from vines. But in order for his produce to be at this stage of growth, what things would a farmer have already done to prepare his crops? List all the things you can think of.

_____

_____

_____

Now suppose you defined your job as "herdsperson." However, under the present circumstances you have "no sheep in the pen and no cattle in the stalls" (v. 17 NIV). How do you think you would feel about yourself? How might you feel about God?

_____

_____

_____

LIVING BY THE BOOK

In the culture of Habakkuk's time, crops and animals were the equivalent of our bank accounts. That's where the money was. People who had neither vineyards, herds, nor olive groves had no means of income. Yet what was the attitude of the writer?

_____

_____

_____

_____

Suppose Habakkuk were writing from your job and culture. Rather than using the imagery of olives, grapes, sheep, and cattle, what terms and comparisons might he have used? Try to rewrite verses 17 and 18 to make the same point, but from the perspective of your own culture.

_____

_____

_____

_____

53

DOING FURTHER CONSULTATION

TODAY'S PASSAGE:
Habakkuk 3:17–19

TIME COMMITMENT:
30 minutes

Consultation involves the use of secondary resources. They can shed light on the text that will help you make more sense out of what you're looking at. You see, we never want to become arrogant in the study process by thinking that we've got all the answers, that the Holy Spirit speaks to us, but He's never spoken to anyone else. The truth of the matter is, thousands of people have walked this road before us. . . . But one word of caution: Never forget the order. First the text of Scripture; then secondary sources" (pp. 243–44).

To review what was said in chapter 34 of *Living by the Book*, it helps to have "tools" to assist you in Bible study after you've observed and interpreted the text to the best of your ability. A good study Bible and an exhaustive concordance are key to Bible study. But in addition, you will probably make good use of a Bible dictionary, Bible handbook, Bible atlas, a good commentary, and other helpful resources. As we learn to consult the right references, our Bible study can progress to a new depth.

Collect all the "tools" you have for Bible study, and again read Habakkuk 3:17–19. You've already used a concordance, so use the other resources to see what you can find out about some of the following things. (You've already answered some of these questions on your own. Now see if you can discover anything new about them.)

What was the significance of olives, grapes, and figs in Bible times?

_____

_____

_____

How important were herds of sheep and cattle?

_____

_____

_____

How bad did things get during times of famine?

_____

_____

_____

What else can you discover about the Babylonians (or "Chaldeans") who were attacking the city?

_____

_____

_____

Speaking of the city of Jerusalem, what would have made it a challenging target for an invading force? Why was it worth the effort?

_____

_____

_____

Based on the words chosen to describe God, what was Habakkuk's intention in describing his Lord?

_____

_____

_____

What other questions do you have about this passage? (Now is the time to check them out.)

_____

_____

_____

54

COMING TO TERMS

TODAY'S PASSAGE:
Book of Habakkuk

———

TIME COMMITMENT:
30 minutes

A 'term' is a key word or phrase that an author uses to make his point. He may use the word repeatedly to give it emphasis. He may place it on display in some prominent verse. He may build a story around it to illustrate its significance. Or he may put it in the mouth of a central character in his narrative. However he signals them, an author wants you to pay attention to his terms, because they are freighted with meaning. Unless you 'come to terms with the terms,' you'll never understand his message" (p. 252).

You've just been through the five keys to Interpretation: Content, Context, Comparison, Culture, and Consultation. In doing so, you've remained in the same passage of Scripture—only three verses, for the most part. But while you're familiarizing yourself with various Bible tools, today's assignment gives you the opportunity to better identify some noteworthy terms used. Since Habakkuk 3:17–19 is a relatively straightforward and simple passage, let's back up and look at some terms found earlier in the book.

Depending on the Bible translation you are using, these terms pop up in various verses. Choose one or more of the following terms, start with its occurrences in Habakkuk, and then use a concordance to see where else it pops up and what conclusions you can draw about its significance.

- Justice/injustice

_____

_____

_____

- Judgment

_____

_____

_____

- Cup (2:16)

_____

_____

_____

- Deliverance

_____

_____

_____

- (Choose another term that looks interesting to you.)

_____

_____

_____

55

FIGURING OUT
THE FIGURATIVE
Some Guidelines

When we come upon figurative language in Scripture, there are a number of things to remember. Here are ten principles taken from chapter 36 of *Living by the Book* as reminders of how to deal with figurative language.

(1) Use the literal sense unless there is some good reason not to.

(2) Use the figurative sense when the passage tells you to do so.

(3) Use the figurative sense if a literal meaning is impossible or absurd.

(4) Use the figurative sense if a literal meaning would involve something immoral.

(5) Use the figurative sense if the expression is an obvious figure of speech.

(6) Use the figurative sense if a literal interpretation goes contrary to the context and scope of the passage.

(7) Use the figurative sense if a literal interpretation goes contrary to the general character and style of the book.

(8) Use the figurative sense if a literal interpretation goes contrary to the plan and purpose of the author.

__(9)__ Use the figurative sense if a literal interpretation involves a contradiction of other Scripture.

__(10)__ Use the figurative sense if a literal interpretation would involve a contradiction in doctrine.

56

FIGURING OUT THE FIGURATIVE

TODAY'S PASSAGE:
Judges 9:9–15

———

TIME COMMITMENT:
20 minutes

The issue here is figurative language. We're all familiar with figures of speech. We use them all the time: 'I could have died of embarrassment.' 'I guess I'll have to face the music.' 'So-and-so is as mad as a hornet.' 'He was bored to tears.' 'Don't let the cat out of the bag.' 'She has a green thumb.' The biblical writers and characters were no different. They laced their material with vivid images, and peculiar ways of speaking" (p. 258).

When you think of parables in the Bible, perhaps Jesus' stories come to mind immediately. Yet He was merely using a literary form that had already existed for centuries.

Read Judges 9:9–15. If you heard this story out of context, what do you think it might mean?

_____

_____

_____

Now go back and put the parable into context. Read Judges 8:28–9:21. What additional information do you discover about the meaning of the story? (If you have questions about names, places, etc., you should know by now how to deal with them.)

_____

_____

_____

Why do you think figurative language was used in this instance?

_____

_____

Do you think the impact of this passage would have been the same if the speaker had used facts in place of his symbolism? Why or why not?

_____

_____

_____

57

FIGURING OUT
THE FIGURATIVE

TODAY'S PASSAGE:
Revelation 17

———

TIME COMMITMENT:
20 minutes

God does not shroud Himself in unknowable mysticism. When He wants to tell us something, He tells us. He doesn't confound us with nonsense. However, He often uses symbolism to make His points. Yet He expects us to read them as symbols, not absurdities" (p. 261).

Perhaps no portion of Scripture is as challenging to interpret as the book of Revelation. The various opinions and speculations about the meaning of this book are numerous. We may never figure out all the symbolism to our satisfaction. Yet at the most basic level, the message of Revelation is usually reasonably clear.

For example, read Revelation 17. As you do, list the symbols and the figurative language you find. After you compile your list, add any of the interpretations you can be sure of. You may have a few blanks remaining, but you should have much of your list filled out. If you read closely, several of the symbols are explained within the text. Others (such as the beasts, the Lamb, etc.) are defined elsewhere in Revelation.

You may not understand everything that's going on, but in the space below, list everything that *is* clear from reading this chapter.

_____

_____

_____

_____

_____

_____

Some people come across figurative language and give up before they even try to understand it. But we hope you have seen that the use of symbolism and figurative language doesn't necessarily prevent comprehension of Scripture. Indeed, many times such symbols can add intrigue and interest to certain sections of the Bible.

Part 3

APPLICATION

FROM INTERPRETATION TO APPLICATION

As you begin the final section of this book, remember that Application is of the utmost importance. You can have learned everything up to this point and done all the exercises. But unless you start to apply what you're learning, your Bible study is essentially in vain. As we have said before, many people focus on Interpretation to the point of missing the benefits of Observation and Application. But the better you get at Observation, the less Interpretation you need. And until you find the proper Applications for your life, your Interpretation is of little practical use.

Nor can we do much in the way of telling you *how* to apply everything you're learning. We all approach Scripture with our own backgrounds, points of view, problems, and interests. God speaks to each of us through His Word, but not necessarily in the same way. A group of people might examine the same passage on any given day, and each one would come away from it with a different response. So it's going to be up to you to take the initiative to pull out from Scripture what's there for you. While we can provide a few guidelines to help you, the bulk of the work is going to be up to you from here on.

We suggest you review the Application section of *Living by the Book* (chapters 39 through 45). We will provide a few new exercises in this workbook, and we'll try to include a lot of application reminders in the Bible book studies that follow.

And as another reminder, here are four substitutes for Application that don't work nearly as well. Be sure to avoid these traps as you approach this final section of learning to live by the Book. (Review them in more detail, if you wish, on pages 285–89 of *Living by the Book*.)

FOUR SUBSTITUTES FOR APPLICATION

(1) We substitute interpretation for application.

(2) We substitute superficial obedience for substantive life-change.

(3) We substitute rationalization for repentance.

(4) We substitute an emotional experience for a volitional decision.

58

THE PROCESS
OF APPLICATION

TODAY'S PASSAGE:
Ecclesiastes 3:1–14

TIME COMMITMENT:
45 minutes

Many Christians are like poor photographs—overexposed and under-developed. They've had plenty of input from the Word of God, but what difference has it made in their lives? Spiritual growth is a commitment to change. And yet, the human heart resists nothing as strongly as it resists change. We will do anything to avoid it" (p. 292).

You might want to review chapter 40 of *Living by the Book* in preparation for the next couple of exercises. The chapter provides four steps to follow in learning to apply Scripture appropriately. In short, they are:

STEP 1   **Know**—We need to know the Scripture text and know ourselves.

STEP 2   **Relate**—We must relate the Word of God to our own experiences.

STEP 3   **Meditate**—We need to pay close attention to the Scriptures, even memorizing them so they will continue to work in our hearts and minds.

STEP 4   **Practice**—The practice of truth should be our primary goal of Bible study.

Read Ecclesiastes 3:1–14 and work your way through these four steps. Use what you've already learned about Observation and Interpretation to examine the passage, knowing it and relating it to your own life. Then meditate on it. (The first eight verses are an excellent portion of Scripture to commit to memory.) Finally, determine at least three ways you can apply what the text is saying. How can you put this text into practice in your life *this week?*

59

THE PROCESS OF APPLICATION

> TODAY'S PASSAGE:
> *Galatians 5:16–26*
>
> ———
>
> TIME COMMITMENT:
> *30 minutes*

W hat is the process of life-change all about? It begins with the Word of God. The Bible is God's divine means of bringing change into our lives. But notice, the Word must first change my life. Then it can begin to change my world" (p. 303).

Following the same four steps of Application described in the previous assignment, this time read Galatians 5:16–26. Paul was contrasting the worst elements of the human condition with the best that God has to offer. Regardless of your spiritual condition, you ought to find something to relate to as you examine this passage.

Using Observation, what are the things you need to *know* about Galatians 5:16–26?

_____

_____

How can you *relate* this passage to your life?

_____

_____

Spend some time to *meditate* on the passage. (Again, all or part of it is good to memorize and retain.)

And finally, in what specific ways can you *practice* what is being taught in this portion of the Bible?

_____

_____

_____

60
NINE QUESTIONS TO ASK

Here are nine questions you can ask as you study any passage of Scripture. They can be of great benefit to help you glean relevant applications for the portion of the Bible you are studying.

(1) Is there an example for me to follow?

(2) Is there a sin to avoid?

(3) Is there a promise to claim?

(4) Is there a prayer to repeat?

(5) Is there a command to obey?

(6) Is there a condition to meet?

(7) Is there a verse to memorize?

(8) Is there an error to mark?

(9) Is there a challenge to face?

If you need help remembering the specifics for any of these questions, review chapter 41 of *Living by the Book*.

61

ASKING THE RIGHT QUESTIONS

TODAY'S PASSAGE:
Ezekiel 33:1–10

———

TIME COMMITMENT:
45 minutes

Application is the most neglected yet the most needed stage in the process. Too much Bible study begins and ends in the wrong place: It begins with Interpretation, and it also ends there. But we've learned that you don't start with the question, What does this mean? but rather, What does this say? Furthermore, you don't end the process by asking, What does this mean? but rather, How does this work? Again, not does it work—but how?" (p. 283).

At first reading, Ezekiel 33:1–10 might seem like little more than God's instructions to one of His prophets—nothing much for someone in the twenty-first century. But remember your process of *knowing* Scripture, *relating* to it, *meditating* on it, and *practicing* it. As you do, bring to your reading the nine questions on the previous page (which we've reprinted below). You should be able to uncover a number of applications that make sense in your life today.

 (1) Is there an example for me to follow?

 (2) Is there a sin to avoid?

 (3) Is there a promise to claim?

 (4) Is there a prayer to repeat?

(5) Is there a command to obey?

(6) Is there a condition to meet?

(7) Is there a verse to memorize?

(8) Is there an error to mark?

(9) Is there a challenge to face?

62

ASKING THE
RIGHT QUESTIONS

> **TODAY'S PASSAGE:**
> *1 Thessalonians 5*
>
> ————
>
> **TIME COMMITMENT:**
> *30 minutes*

The Bible was not written to satisfy your curiosity; it was written to transform your life. The ultimate goal of Bible study, then, is not to do something to the Bible, but to allow the Bible to do something to you, so truth becomes tangent to life" (p. 284).

Using your list of nine questions again, work your way through 1 Thessalonians 5. This passage should contain considerably more examples than the previous one as responses to your nine questions. But just because many "obvious" observations pop out, don't forget to meditate on the chapter and see if there aren't other, less obvious lessons and applications. Again, we've reproduced the nine questions here for your convenience. We suggest you use this list for future Bible studies where you're looking for good practical applications.

 (1) Is there an example for me to follow?

 (2) Is there a sin to avoid?

 (3) Is there a promise to claim?

 (4) Is there a prayer to repeat?

 (5) Is there a command to obey?

Is there a condition to meet?

 Is there a verse to memorize?

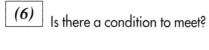 Is there an error to mark?

 Is there a challenge to face?

63

CULTURES IN CONTEXT

TODAY'S PASSAGE:
Genesis 25:19–34; 27:1–46

———

TIME COMMITMENT:
60 minutes

We saw the importance of context to Interpretation. Now we discover its importance to Application. We've got to understand the ancient culture. The more we know about the culture in which a passage was written and to which it was originally applied, the more accurate will be our understanding and the more we'll be able to make use of it in our own cultural setting. But that's not all. We also must understand our own culture. Just as we seek insight into the ancient context, we need to seek insight into our own" (pp. 311–12).

The conflict between Jacob and Esau may be a rather familiar story to many of us. Yet do you really understand the significance of the red stew incident (Genesis 25:27–34)? What was the big deal about Isaac's blessing of Jacob instead of Esau (27:27–40)?

We can get a sense of what's happening in these accounts, but we won't fully understand it until we get a clear grasp on the culture of the time. See what you can find out that can help you better understand this story. Consider looking for additional information about *birthrights* and the rights of the *firstborn*. Begin by seeking out other biblical sources where these issues are discussed. When you've exhausted all your scriptural sources, then look in other resources (commentaries, Bible dictionaries, etc.). Record your discoveries below.

_____

_____

_____

_____

_____

_____

When you have a good understanding of the biblical culture and the significance of the events, you are only half finished. That was then. This is now. As you gain a better understanding of Jacob's and Esau's dilemma, what lessons are there for today's culture? What do these stories have to tell us as parents about favoritism, sibling rivalry, birth order, etc.? Put some thought into these issues and record your insights.

_____

_____

_____

_____

_____

_____

64

CULTURES
IN CONTEXT

TODAY'S PASSAGE:
Mark 1:21–45

TIME COMMITMENT:
60 minutes

The point is that the Word of God is eternal and unchanging, but our world is not. Therefore, living out God's truth demands that we plug it into our particular set of circumstances. But please note: We do not change the truth to fit our cultural agenda. Rather, we change our application of the truth in light of our needs" (p. 311).

There are dozens of Gospel accounts of the miracles of Jesus. He would walk down the street healing the sick, casting out demons, raising the dead, and so forth. But have you ever tried to imagine what it would be like to live in that culture?

Read Mark 1:21–45. After you do, try to see what else you can find out about that society. We suggest you focus on two specific social problems in the culture of Jesus' day: leprosy and demon possession. What would it be like to walk down the street and encounter either or both of these things in the people you meet?

_____

_____

_____

_____

Again, begin with Scripture itself to see what you can find. Only after you have found what you can about the disease of leprosy and the issue of demon possession, turn to other sources. How did the people in this culture deal with such problems?

_____

_____

_____

And again, what is the lesson for our own culture? We don't usually see a lot of people afflicted with leprosy or evil spirits. But how can we apply this portion of Scripture to our own lives?

_____

_____

_____

_____

65

STATING PRINCIPLES FROM SCRIPTURE

TODAY'S PASSAGE:
Leviticus 16

TIME COMMITMENT:
60 minutes

Crafting useful and accurate principles requires accurate understanding of the text and perceptive insight into our own context. Here are several questions to help you develop and apply biblically sound principles.

(1) What can you discover about the original context in which this passage was written and applied?

(2) Given that original context, what does this text mean?

(3) What fundamental, universal truths are presented in this passage?

(4) Can you state that truth in a simple sentence or two, a statement that anyone could understand?

(5) What issues in your own culture and your own situation does this truth address?

(6) What are the implications of this principle when applied to your life and the world around you? What changes does it require? What values does it reinforce? What difference does it make?" (pp. 322–23).

In addition to the six questions above, keep in mind that: (1) principles should correlate with the general teaching of Scripture; (2) principles should speak to the needs, interests, questions, and problems of real life today; and (3) principles should indicate a course of action.

If you need to, review chapter 43 of *Living by the Book*. Then see how well you can do at formulating some principles based on today's passage.

Leviticus 16 describes the procedure the Israelites followed on the annual Day of Atonement—what is now known as Yom Kippur and remains the holiest of the Jewish special days. Use your skills of Observation and Interpretation to examine the text. Figure out the significance of this event to the ancient Hebrew culture, and consider how your own culture thinks about God.

Finally, see if you can create some principles from this passage that might apply to your own relationship with God, or to today's Christian community as a whole.

66

STATING PRINCIPLES FROM SCRIPTURE

TODAY'S PASSAGE:
2 Peter 3

TIME COMMITMENT:
60 minutes

If you can discern principles from your study of Scripture, you'll have some powerful tools to help you apply biblical truth. You'll bridge the gap between the ancient world and your own situation with the timeless truth of God's Word. . . . If we stock up on principles from Scripture, we'll have a powerful set of resources to deal with the situations of life. You see, principles enable us to multiply truth. One interpretation; many applications. We may not have a specific verse to plug into the circumstances of the moment. But we can still navigate a godly path by extrapolating from the truth we already know" (pp. 318, 322).

Refer to the previous assignment to review the questions and groundwork for stating principles from Scripture. Then, for today's assignment, take a look at 2 Peter 3. With the recent uproar concerning the Millennium and the Y2K bug, try to state some good-to-remember principles from Peter's writing concerning Jesus' second coming.

67

A PROCESS OF LIFE-CHANGE

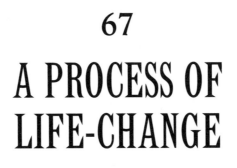

TODAY'S PASSAGE:
Your Choice

———

TIME COMMITMENT:
60 minutes

Too much 'application' stays at the level of good intentions because we talk about the end of the journey without specifying when, where, and how we're going to take the first step" (p. 325).

Chapter 44 of *Living by the Book* deals with the essential commitment to following up Bible study—Observation, Interpretation, and Application—with the changes we know need to be made in our lives. By this point in the workbook, perhaps you have felt the gentle nudging (or perhaps the outright prodding) of the Holy Spirit to address a particular aspect of your life where you desire to see positive change.

Don't forget the three steps for converting your good intentions into action:

(1) Make a decision to change. Decide exactly what you desire to do, and then determine your general objectives. Be as specific as possible.

(2) Come up with a plan. Stay specific as you decide the best way you can accomplish the objectives you have set up.

(3) Follow through. Don't put it off. Initiate your plan right away and see it through to completion. Use a checklist, evaluate your progress regularly, and report to an accountability group to ensure you don't get sidetracked or bogged down.

Choose any area of life-change you wish. As you allow the Word of God to teach, rebuke, correct, and train in righteousness (2 Timothy 3:16), you can experience positive changes that you never thought possible.

Part 4

PUTTING IT
ALL TOGETHER

INTRODUCTION

So far in this workbook we've introduced a number of different Bible study methods grouped in the categories of Observation, Interpretation, and Application. To illustrate each one, we've suggested a portion of Scripture to let you accustom yourself to that particular method.

But now that you have some of those methods under your belt and have had a bit of practice, we're going to reverse the process. Rather than introducing Scripture to learn the methods, we're going to combine the methods to learn Scripture. We're going to spend thirty days in Ruth, and then in James, using various study methods we've seen to help us get more from God's Word.

In each day's assignment, you'll receive a suggested method of study. But please use our outline only as a suggested *guideline*. If you want to rearrange the order of our lessons, please do. Most of the activities can be completed in a half hour or so. If you want to take longer (or shorter), feel free to do so. If you see something not in our daily studies, or if you have a hankering to go off on a tangent we haven't pursued, that's all part of studying Scripture on your own. You may not even want to examine Ruth or James at this point, but we've purposely avoided pulling too much from either of these books in other sections of the workbook so you can have the opportunity to approach these sections of Scripture with a fresh perspective.

We've divided the following studies into approximately equal sections for Observation, Interpretation, and Application. However, don't forget that the better you do at Observation, the more natural the rest of your study should be. If you're not quite ready to move on when we do, don't feel rushed.

The books of Ruth and James are quite different, but you'll use the same methods to examine each one. And remember, this isn't a race. If an assignment doesn't make sense to you, spend some time reviewing the principle in this workbook or in *Living by the Book*. If it takes a day to catch up, you'll be that much better off the next day. It's much more important that you make gradual, regular progress rather than merely "getting another page done."

May God bless your study of His Word in these activities and in your lifetime of living by the Book.

68

BOOK OF RUTH
Day 1

Yͭou're going to read the Book of Ruth repeatedly and patiently over the course of the following month, and we suggest you use a number of different translations as you do. Read it straight through today to get familiar with the story, the settings, and the characters. List the characters, the places mentioned, and any questions you have. Don't worry too much about what you don't know at this point. You'll have twenty-nine days after today to piece together the holes in your perspective.

Characters

_____
_____
_____
_____
_____

Places

_____
_____
_____
_____
_____

Questions for Follow-Up

_____
_____
_____
_____
_____

BOOK OF RUTH
Day 2

Read Ruth 1 imaginatively. For example:

- If this were all you knew about the story , whose story would you say this was?

_____

_____

Put yourself in Naomi's place. Consider:

- Why did you leave home in the first place?

_____

_____

- In your attempt to make things better, what happened?

_____

_____

- How would you feel about yourself?

_____

_____

- How would you feel about God?

_____

_____

- How would you feel about Ruth?

_____

_____

Now put yourself in Ruth's place.

- Would you have made the same choice to leave your home and go with Naomi? Why or why not?

_____

_____

- How would you feel to not only have to care for yourself, but also to take care of an older woman in a country strange to you?

_____

_____

- What do you think would be your biggest fears and concerns?

_____

_____

- What else would you be feeling?

_____

_____

BOOK OF RUTH
Day 3

Read Ruth 2 selectively. Ask yourself the six questions:

- Who are the people in the text (and what's the significance of leaving behind four of the people you began with in Ruth 1)?

_____

_____

- What's happening in this text? If this were the plot of a movie of the week, what might you expect to happen next?

_____

_____

- Where is the action taking place? Is the location important in any way?

_____

_____

- When was this story taking place? What would have been significant about, say, the role of women during this time in history?

_____

_____

- Why did Ruth volunteer to help Naomi? Why did Boaz volunteer to help Ruth? Why did Naomi encourage Ruth? Why do we seem to get so much insight into the characters of these people?

_____

_____

- So what? What do you think is the significance of all the action taking place?

_____

_____

BOOK OF RUTH
Day 4

Read Ruth 3 meditatively. This can be a troublesome passage if we don't give it sufficient thought. As we pointed out in *Living by the Book,* some people read this portion of Scripture and respond with winks and elbow pokes, suggesting that Ruth acted inappropriately (p. 237).

Later on you'll be asked to consult other references to see what is taking place culturally. But for now, meditate on Ruth 3 (as well as other portions of the book) and see what you can learn about the people involved. Your assignment is a single essay question: When Ruth washed, dressed in her best clothes, and sneaked out to see Boaz in the middle of the night, do you think it was to sleep with him? Why or why not?

_____

_____

_____

_____

_____

_____

_____

_____

_____

_____

_____

BOOK OF RUTH
Day 5

Read Ruth 4 purposefully. The Book of Ruth is a literary work of art, so its literary structures are well worth examining. For example:

- What is significant about the biographical structure of the book? Why did the writer place so much importance on the people involved?

_____

_____

- What is significant about the geographical structure? Why does the action in Ruth move from Judah, to Moab, and back to Judah?

_____

_____

- Historically, why is this story important? (You don't really find out until the very end of chapter 4.)

_____

_____

- Is anything important about the chronology of the book? For example, suppose you were to graph the emotional tone of the book from beginning to end. What would your graph look like?

_____

_____

- From an ideological standpoint, what would you say is the central theme of the Book of Ruth?

_____

_____

BOOK OF RUTH
Day 6

Read the Book of Ruth telescopically. As the book begins, what events are taking place on a national level?

_____

_____

_____

_____

As the book ends, what information is provided that again brings the importance of the story to a national level for the nation of Judah?

_____

_____

_____

_____

Why, then, does this account of Naomi, Ruth, and Boaz appear "under the microscope" of Scripture? Why does the author zoom in to reveal so much about the lives of three seemingly insignificant people?

_____

_____

_____

_____

BOOK OF RUTH
Day 7

Read the Book of Ruth prayerfully. Don't expect to find a lot of fancy prayers written out to repeat, but note the language used by the characters. Specifically, record all the places you find the phrase "May the Lord . . ." or something to that effect.

_____

_____

_____

_____

_____

_____

_____

Also spend some time thinking how your outlook on life might be different if more people regularly prayed that the Lord would do good things for you. And while you're at it, how good are you at blessing other people on a regular basis?

_____

_____

_____

_____

_____

_____

BOOK OF RUTH
Day 8

Read the Book of Ruth looking for things that are repeated and/or emphasized. Remember that emphasis can be determined by the amount of space allotted to a story, a stated purpose, the designated order of events, or movement from the lesser to the greater or vice versa. For example, why is Ruth such a "feel good" book in spite of all the tragedy at its beginning? Where does it get such a positive emphasis?

_____
_____
_____
_____
_____
_____

Things that are repeated can include terms or phrases, characters, incidents and circumstances, or patterns of behavior. To get you started, we suggest you look for acts of faith. As you read through the book, you should find considerable repetition. Then see how many other important repetitions you can find.

BOOK OF RUTH
Day 9

Read the Book of Ruth looking for things that are alike or unlike. The book is not a source of many outright metaphors and similes. But consider the characters themselves and what they represent. To whom are they compared? How do they compare with each other? Also review how irony can be used to point out obvious contrasts in Scripture, and look for examples from the story of Ruth.

_____

_____

_____

_____

_____

_____

_____

_____

_____

BOOK OF RUTH
Day 10

Read the Book of Ruth looking for things that are related. These connections might be made through movement from the general to the specific, questions and answers, or cause and effect. You'll probably find more examples from the cause and effect category than the other two. But read carefully, looking for how certain people or events are brought into relation to one another. List all the examples you find.

_____

_____

_____

_____

_____

_____

_____

_____

BOOK OF RUTH
Day 11

At this point, we're shifting the emphasis from Observation to Interpretation. You'll be looking at many similar aspects of the Book of Ruth, but with more of an emphasis on understanding and making sense of what you're reading rather than simply observing.

Let's begin by considering how the Book of Ruth would be classified in terms of literary genre. We would suggest that Ruth belongs to the biography and narrative categories. Now that you've read through the book several times, review the list on pages 115–116 and see if you agree.

As we approach this type of material, we need to ask the following questions. You will already have answered some of them. Focus on what is new, but also consider that additional thought on already studied material frequently provides new insights.

What is the plot? What movement is there in the story?

_____

_____

Who is the cast of characters? How are they presented? What roles do they play?

_____

_____

How do the characters relate to each other and to God? What progress or regress do they make? Do they fail?

_____

_____

In what ways are the characters individuals, and in what ways are they representative of others? What do you like or dislike about them? What would you do in their places?

_____

_____

What questions does this story raise? How do the characters deal with the unavoidable problems of life? What do they discover about God?

_____

_____

BOOK OF RUTH
Day 12

Read the Book of Ruth again, focusing exclusively on the *content*. When you finish, review the list of questions you wrote out on Day 1. By now you should have answered several of them. However, others may remain unanswered.

With all the examination of Ruth you've done to this point, you're likely to have added to your list of questions. If so, good! List everything else you want to know about this intriguing book. You still have ample time to come to some logical conclusions concerning the answers you seek.

_____

_____

_____

_____

_____

_____

_____

_____

_____

.

BOOK OF RUTH
Day 13

Spend a day considering the historical context of the Book of Ruth. You know it took place "in the days when the judges governed" (1:1), but what does that mean? You'll find the answer in the Book of Judges. For today's study, back up one Bible book and read Judges. You may want to go back and do an in-depth study of that fascinating book later, but today remain focused on the historical perspectives. For example:

- How did Israel relate to the nations around it?

_____

_____

- What kind of leadership structure did Israel have?

_____

_____

- This was after Moses and before the prophets. How did God communicate with His people?

_____

_____

- Do you find any other bold women who might have inspired Ruth and Naomi?

_____

_____

- What was the spiritual condition of Israel during this time?

_____

_____

- What other significant historical insights do you find?

_____

_____

BOOK OF RUTH
Day 14

The Book of Ruth takes place in two primary locations: Bethlehem (in Judah) and Moab. Today's assignment is to get a geographical context for this passage of Scripture by seeing what you can discover about these two places. First use a concordance and see what you can find out from Scripture alone. (You may not be able to look up all the references, but examine enough of a sampling to discover some patterns.) Then, if you wish, consult other sources to see what they have to say about the significance of these two locations in the Bible.

My discoveries about Moab

_____

_____

_____

My discoveries about Bethlehem

_____

_____

_____

BOOK OF RUTH
Day 15

Read the Book of Ruth to get the theological context. Based on your knowledge of Old Testament Scripture, would you make any connections between the geography and the theology of certain nations? In other words, did various religions tend to be localized within certain countries?

_____

_____

_____

Now that you know a little about Moab (Ruth's home) and Bethlehem (Naomi's home), what would you expect Naomi to know about God? What about Ruth?

_____

_____

_____

From a theological standpoint, what problems might you expect in Ruth's and Naomi's relationship? What differences, if any, do you find?

_____

_____

_____

How would you evaluate the spiritual commitment of Naomi? Of Boaz? Of Ruth?

_____

_____

_____

BOOK OF RUTH
Day 16

U se the technique of comparison to interpret the Book of Ruth. See how this portion of Scripture stacks up against others. For example, Ruth is frequently perceived as a "quaint" story of romance. But how many other potential brides can you find who were as aggressive?

_____

_____

_____

How does the Ruth/Boaz relationship compare with other Old Testament couples you know about?

_____

_____

_____

Can you find other biblical in-laws? If so, how do they compare to Ruth and Naomi?

_____

_____

_____

Other comparisons and observations:

_____

_____

_____

BOOK OF RUTH
Day 17

The Book of Ruth is filled with customs that can only be understood after an examination of the cultural context. For your assignments the next several days, use other resources to bolster your accumulating knowledge of the biblical text.

Today, determine what was involved with harvesting crops during Ruth's lifetime. You should know by now that Ruth was involved with first the barley harvest (1:22) and then the wheat harvest (2:23). References are made to gleaning (2:2), winnowing (3:2), threshing (3:2), and reaping (2:3). At some point, apparently, sheaves were involved (2:7).

Yet even after observing all these facts, it is difficult to interpret them without some additional help. Find out what these terms mean, and determine the process of converting the growing plants into food for the people.

If you finish and have some time remaining, see what you can find out about what it was like to be a childless widow in Ruth's culture. What were the physical challenges? The social considerations? The emotional mindset?

BOOK OF RUTH
Day 18

In addition to our need to know about the importance of harvesting in Ruth's culture, which you looked at yesterday, there are additional things in the Book of Ruth that are even less familiar to us. Have your Bible resources handy as you take a closer look at Ruth 4. For one thing, why was Ruth's closest relative willing to let Boaz have Elimelech's inheritance? It seems he would have taken the field (v. 4) until he found out that a wife went with it (v. 5). What did he mean when he said, "I cannot redeem it for myself, because I would jeopardize my own inheritance" (v. 6)?

_____

_____

_____

_____

_____

And while you're at it, what was the deal with the sandal? See what you can find out about the custom of transferring a sandal to seal a business deal (4:7–8).

_____

_____

_____

_____

BOOK OF RUTH
Day 19

Continue your pursuit of cultural context, today by doing some research concerning Ruth's and Boaz's nighttime rendezvous (Ruth 3). You should have examined the matter from a scriptural, observational perspective on Day 4. Today do some consulting to see if other Bible scholars agree with your observations. How are we to interpret Ruth's actions?

_____

_____

_____

_____

_____

_____

_____

_____

BOOK OF RUTH
Day 20

This is the final day we're allotting to Interpretation, so use it as a "free day" to pursue whatever issues you wish. If you still have some pressing questions, this is the day to search for answers. Even if your list of questions has dwindled to nothing, why not spend the day poring over some different Bible versions, new commentaries, Bible handbooks, or related materials to find out if there are important facts you've still overlooked? Remember that Scripture speaks to different people in different ways. Someone else might make some basic connections that you haven't yet discovered in your examination of the Book of Ruth.

BOOK OF RUTH
Day 21

You may remember that the four steps to effective Application of Scripture are to know, relate, meditate on, and practice what you find in the text. By now you should know the Book of Ruth very well. So your assignment today is to shift your thinking from Interpretation to Application as you begin to relate what you've been reading to your current experiences.

Read the Book of Ruth and list all the portions that trigger something that you personally have faced, or may be currently facing. For now, keep your list general. Later we will write principles that arise from Ruth and determine some applications that are more specific. Today simply look for advice or examples from Ruth, Naomi, and Boaz that could make a difference in your life if you applied what you are learning.

WHAT I'M LEARNING FROM THE BOOK OF RUTH   **HOW I CAN APPLY THIS TO MY LIFE**

BOOK OF RUTH
Day 22

Today we want to meditate on the Book of Ruth. This will be from an Application standpoint. (You had the opportunity to read meditatively on Day 4.) Your goal today should be to dwell on the passages in the Book of Ruth you feel are particularly important to you. You should know the book quite well by now, so zero in on what you feel is most essential and spend some time thinking about what it really means to you.

Meditating on Scripture is an investment in your future. While you're here, while you have time, you can do more than merely read words on a page. As you meditate on Scripture, God's Word is planted in your mind for future reference. That's why we encourage you to commit to memory what you find so helpful. Scripture memory allows you "around-the-clock" access to the passages of the Bible you find most applicable to your life.

BOOK OF RUTH
Day 23

You probably remember the nine questions we used to help us apply Scripture to our own lives. In this assignment and the next, we will go through the Book of Ruth using these questions to see what else we can discover. You will have already answered some of these questions to a certain degree, but keep looking for additional insight. Today we'll focus on the first five questions, and the next assignment will continue with the final four.

Read the Book of Ruth again and ask yourself:

- Is there an example for me to follow?

_____

_____

_____

- Is there a sin to avoid?

_____

_____

_____

- Is there a promise to claim?

_____

_____

_____

- Is there a prayer to repeat?

_____

_____

_____

- Is there a command to obey?

_____

_____

_____

BOOK OF RUTH
Day 24

This assignment continues the previous one. Here are the other four of the nine questions to help you apply Scripture to your life. Read the Book of Ruth again, answering these questions as you get to relevant portions.

- Is there a condition to meet?

- Is there a verse to memorize?

- Is there an error to mark?

- Is there a challenge to face?

BOOK OF RUTH
Day 25

The next few assignments will ask you to look for different ways you might apply the things you've been learning about the Book of Ruth. Let's start by considering what's there for men to learn. Perhaps you've noticed the popularity of the Book of Ruth for women's studies. But why don't you see more men's groups sitting around discussing this particular portion of Scripture? Is it irrelevant for men? Spend today reading the Book of Ruth and recording the specific ways you think men might apply what's in this book. Remember that you need to be well aware of Ruth's culture, as well as your own. And if you want to suggest principles that can be stated from the text, do so as well.

Applications for Men

Principles to Live By

BOOK OF RUTH
Day 26

In the last assignment you looked for male-oriented applications from the Book of Ruth. Today see what you can apply to the issue of suffering. Usually we turn to Job or to Paul's struggles to make sense of the suffering that takes place in our lives. But do you think Ruth and Naomi would have anything to say about the topic? Read the Book of Ruth again, this time noting any applications and/or principles that might be helpful the next time you face suffering in your own life.

Applications for Dealing with Suffering

_____

_____

_____

_____

_____

Principles to Live By

_____

_____

_____

_____

_____

BOOK OF RUTH
Day 27

Today we continue to search for practical applications from the Book of Ruth. Read the book again, this time paying special attention to the "coincidences" that take place. These may be positive or negative, but look closely. Sometimes we read Scripture in retrospect, knowing how everything turns out, and we overlook the significance of certain events. Put yourself in the place of the characters facing their circumstances as they occur. You should see clearly how God was at work in the "luck"—good or bad—of Ruth, Naomi, and Boaz. Then, as an exercise in Application, determine how the same things might be true in your own life.

Applications for How God Works in the "Coincidences" of Life

_____

_____

_____

_____

_____

_____

Principles to Live By

_____

_____

_____

_____

_____

By the way, if this is an issue you find interesting, read the Book of Esther sometime and list all the instances where "coincidental" timing plays a key role in the plot. You'll be amazed at how many you find.

_____

_____

_____

_____

_____

BOOK OF RUTH
Day 28

Continue searching for principles from the Book of Ruth. Today, however, you may go your own direction. With only a couple more activities after this one, feel free to delve into the Book of Ruth as you wish. Do you think we've exhausted the book? We've hardly touched on applications concerning love, commitment, the importance of maintaining a good reputation, service to others, integrity in the workplace, respect for women, rewards for faithfulness, and so forth. Choose one or more of these things, or something else you want to pursue, and create some principles that will be useful to you in the future.

BOOK OF RUTH
Day 29

If you wish, spend today as you did yesterday in searching for worthwhile principles from the Book of Ruth. But if you want a creative alternative, consider looking at the process of harvesting as a symbol of Bible study itself. After telling the parable of the sower (Mark 4:1–20), Jesus explained to His disciples, "The sower sows the word" (v. 14). God's Word goes out as seed, and seed that falls on good soil multiplies many times (v. 20).

You took a look at the Old Testament process of harvesting grain on Day 17. Do you see any parallels in this process and the process of Bible study you've practiced in this workbook? If you enjoy symbolism and analogies, see how many comparisons you can make between these two processes. If not, do something else!

_____

_____

_____

_____

_____

_____

BOOK OF RUTH
Day 30

When many people speak of the Book of Ruth, they talk as if it's simply a cute Old Testament love story. Would your study confirm this, or have you found more to the book than you originally assumed?

_____

_____

_____

This is the final day we're devoting to the Book of Ruth, although you should feel free to continue your study as long as you wish. And perhaps you'll begin to notice things in your life that send you back to this text on a regular basis from now on.

For this final assignment, devote some time to any life-change aspects of this Bible book. Think of the spiritual challenges you are facing and the things you would like to improve about yourself. Then consider how, if at all, the Book of Ruth might speak to those things. Perhaps the Ruth text will remind you of other Scripture that is more applicable to your situation. But whatever you decide to do today, remember that no Bible study is complete until you have applied it to your own life in some way.

69
BOOK OF JAMES
Day 1

It shouldn't take long to notice that reading the book of James is quite different from reading the Book of Ruth. Not only is it a New Testament book rather than an Old Testament one, but the style and purpose are quite different.

Begin your study by reading the book straight through. Read thoughtfully. Remember to approach a new section of Scripture as a detective. Your intent today should be to cover the whole "scene," but be sure to make mental notes of things you want to come back to and check out more closely. Also jot down questions you will want to answer during the next month as you study this passage more closely.

Initial Observations

_____
_____
_____
_____
_____
_____

Questions for Follow-Up

_____
_____
_____
_____
_____
_____

BOOK OF JAMES
Day 2

Read through the book of James again, this time reading selectively. Answer the six initial questions:

Who is wrote this material? (James was a popular New Testament name. Which one was this author of this book? Or can you tell?)

_____

_____

_____

What is the argument being made in this book? The author addresses a number of issues, but what is his primary theme?

_____

_____

_____

Where was the author as he wrote? Where were his readers?

_____

_____

_____

When was the author writing? What was going on in his world during this time?

_____

_____

_____

Why did the author say what he did? Why is his message important? Why does his writing style seem so different than, say, the letters of Paul? (Add your own whys as you go along.)

_____

_____

_____

Wherefore? (So what?) What's going to happen if you begin to practice everything the author challenges you to do?

_____

_____

_____

BOOK OF JAMES
Day 3

Read James 1 imaginatively. At this point you should be only observing the text. Later you will do some consultation to find out more about what was happening during this part of church history, but an important clue is provided in James 1:1. The faithful people of God are "dispersed abroad" and James's letter begins with a challenge to endure trials.

Put yourself in the place of someone forced to move away suddenly from your usual friends, community, and church. You're in a new place where worship isn't a priority—in fact, many people are hostile toward your beliefs. Your life is in complete turmoil.

Read James 1 with this mind-set. Make notes of everything you would find significant under such circumstances.

_____

_____

_____

_____

_____

_____

BOOK OF JAMES
Day 4

In James 2 the author makes some bold statements about the importance of "works," which can be confusing if sufficient thought isn't devoted to this matter. You may know that Paul wrote: "For by grace you have been saved through faith; and that not of yourselves, it is the gift of God; not as a result of works, so that no one may boast" (Ephesians 2:8–9).

Is James contradicting Paul in this portion of his book? At first reading, it may sound as if he is. Yet we have confidence that the Bible contains no contradictions—that it is a single, cohesive unit even though many different authors and styles are included.

Your assignment today is to read James 2 meditatively. If James and Paul are not saying different things, then what conclusions can we draw about the connection between faith and works?

BOOK OF JAMES
Day 5

Read James 3 looking for things that are alike and unlike. List your findings below. Remember to look for similes and metaphors (which shouldn't be hard in this case). Also note the occurrences of the word *but*.

Don't get lazy in today's assignment. The part of the chapter about the tongue is going to be rich in examples and can require much attention. But don't overlook other things that are alike and/or unlike. (For example, look for at least two kinds of "wisdom" in verses 13–18.)

BOOK OF JAMES
Day 6

Read James 4 looking for things that are related. As a reminder, below are a few things to look for. You may not find them all in every passage of Scripture, but you should find several good examples in this chapter of James.

Movement from the General to the Specific

_____

_____

_____

_____

_____

_____

Questions and Answers

_____

_____

_____

_____

_____

_____

Cause and Effect

_____

_____

_____

_____

_____

_____

BOOK OF JAMES
Day 7

Read James 5 purposefully. This is the close of his letter, so he should be emphasizing the things he has been writing about. His purpose should be clear by now. Look for grammatical as well as literary structures used by the author to make his point. Again, here are some reminders of what to look for.

GRAMMATICAL STRUCTURES
Verbs
Subject and Object
Modifiers
Prepositional phrases
Connectives

LITERARY STRUCTURES
Biographical structure
Geographic structure
Historical structure
Chronological structure
Ideological structure

Which of these methods (or others you can think of) does James use in this chapter to get across his purpose? (Hint: You might want to start with the couple of biographical figures mentioned in this chapter, which are easy to find. As you look for these, you can also be searching for other relevant structures.)

_____

_____

_____

_____

_____

_____

BOOK OF JAMES
Day 8

Now that you've done a chapter-by-chapter examination of the book of James, read straight through again. As you do, make a note of things that are repeated. Look for terms, phrases, and clauses that keep coming up. What incidents or circumstances are noted more than once? Can you find any patterns or parallels that show up in different places? How about Old Testament passages repeated in the New Testament text? (You should find four or five.)

Read slowly and carefully, and list your findings below.

_____

_____

_____

_____

_____

_____

_____

_____

_____

BOOK OF JAMES
Day 9

Read the book of James looking for things that are true to life. Remember that you're still in the Observation stage. You need not concern yourself yet with Interpretation or Application. Simply list the things that seem to reflect your own life experiences.

(By the way, James should be one of the easiest parts of the Bible for this activity. It is filled with good, practical advice for everyday living. Very little Interpretation is needed because the instructions are straightforward and clear. If anyone complains that the Bible is too hard to understand because of all the theological content, suggest that he or she start a study in James.)

_____

_____

_____

_____

_____

_____

_____

_____

BOOK OF JAMES
Day 10

Today you should continue the Observation portion of the James study. Use your own discretion as to which specific portions you would like to pursue. And as we told you in the Ruth study, be sure to complete your Observation before continuing. If it takes several more days, it's better to take that time now, before moving into Interpretation and Application. Never rush the Observation of Scripture. When you take your time and glean all you can from observing the text, you won't be sorry later.

What other new observations can you make from the book of James?

_____

_____

_____

_____

_____

_____

_____

_____

BOOK OF JAMES
Day 11

When you're ready to move from Observation to Interpretation, do a fresh read-through of the book of James for content. You've been reading to observe all you can, and you probably are beginning to know the text fairly well. But now turn your attention to the matters you feel need interpretation. Make a list of everything you find where the content isn't as clear as you might desire. This list should become the focus of your study for the next several days.

_____

_____

_____

_____

_____

_____

_____

_____

_____

_____

BOOK OF JAMES
Day 12

Refer to the chart of "Literary Genres of the Bible" on pages 115–116. You'll see that the book of James is listed under "Exposition." Read through James again and see how you think it stacks up to each of the criteria listed in the chart. List specific examples where possible.

The characteristics of expository literature are:

- Carefully reasoned argument or explanation

- Well organized

- Logical flow

- Terms are crucial

- Builds to a logical, compelling climax

- The aim is agreement and action

BOOK OF JAMES
Day 13

Read the book of James for context. Below are the things you should be looking for, yet don't expect to find examples of all these things in every portion of Scripture.

Literary Context

How does the literary content of this book fit into the context of Scripture?

_____

_____

_____

Historical Context

How do the events in this book relate to the other historical occurrences of this time period?

_____

_____

_____

Cultural Context

How does what you know about James's culture help you interpret the book? (We'll get more specific about cultural aspects later.)

_____

_____

_____

Geographic Context

Is anything in the book more significant because of the location of the author and/or readers of his work?

_____

_____

_____

Theological Context

What did this author know about God? What was the relationship of his readers to God? How much Scripture did they have access to? What other religions and worldviews were competing for influence?

_____

_____

_____

BOOK OF JAMES
Day 14

Today's assignment is to choose some of the terms in James for a comparative study (comparing Scripture with other Scripture). Use a concordance and search for other uses of one or more key themes in James. For example, the topic of joy comes up early in James (1:2). In *Living by the Book* we saw how *joy* was also a key theme in Philippians (pp. 253–54). You might begin by continuing to see what Scripture says about *joy*, or you can select a different theme from James. There are abundant choices for you to pursue. Below are just a few possibilities from the first chapter of James alone!

Patience	Doubt	Lust
Faith	Trials	Temptation
Endurance	Maturity	Anger
Religion	Crowns	Sin
Firstfruits	Righteousness	Humility

BOOK OF JAMES
Day 15

On Day 2 when you were answering the Observation questions (who? what? where? etc.), the authorship of James came into question. Of all the different New Testament men named James, which was responsible for this book?

_____

At the observational stage, you might not have gathered enough evidence to find a satisfactory answer. But now, as you begin to interpret what you have observed, you can pull out some other sources for consultation. Today, check a number of handbooks, commentaries, and so forth, to see what other people say.

As is the case for several books of the Bible, you may find varying opinions as to who should be credited with authorship. Don't just check a single source and move on. Do enough searching to discover a couple of possibilities, and read the arguments in defense of each one.

And while you're at it, see what else you can find out about the author of this book. Once you determine which James is the correct one, what else can you discover about him? How does this information help you interpret what he had to say?

_____
_____
_____
_____
_____
_____
_____
_____

BOOK OF JAMES
Day 16

The next few assignments will encourage you to do some consulting with other sources in order to get a better grasp of the culture at the time James was written. As you learn to understand the cultural significance of some of these things, you can then begin to compare and contrast them with those of your own culture.

For example, today see what you can discover about social structure in this society. What was the "pecking order" in the Roman Empire? How were non-Romans viewed? What kind of structure was being advocated in Christian writings? What was the structure within the church?

_____

_____

_____

_____

_____

_____

_____

_____

_____

_____

BOOK OF JAMES
Day 17

Today use comparison (of Scripture to other Scripture), followed by consultation of other sources to see what you can find out about the cultural practice of anointing with oil (James 5:14). When would this be done? What was the significance? What is the earliest instance you can find where this was done? Does it have any value in contemporary culture?

_____

_____

_____

_____

_____

_____

_____

_____

BOOK OF JAMES
Day 18

Reread James 3 with the culture in mind. Again note the metaphors James used to describe the tongue. They are clear and simple enough for all of us to comprehend, but consider the effect on people who regularly traveled by ship, who daily might have placed a bit in a horse's mouth, or who got their water from wells. How would James's choice of metaphors work with such people?

_____

_____

_____

_____

_____

_____

Now suppose James were writing to people in your own culture. Do you think he would use the same examples? If not, what are three other items he might choose to get our attention? (For example, the tongue might be like a computer virus, because one little quirk can invalidate an entire file [or disk] of valuable information.)

_____

_____

_____

_____

_____

_____

BOOK OF JAMES
Day 19

Perhaps you have noticed the variety of terms James used to refer to God. Today see what you can find out about each one. Do they mean essentially the same thing? If so, why be so diverse when writing?

For example, here are a few to get you started.

Father of lights (1:17)

Our God and Father (1:27)

Lawgiver and Judge (4:12)

Lord of Sabaoth [or "Almighty God," depending on your translation] (5:4)

BOOK OF JAMES
Day 20

This is another choose-your-own-assignment day. It's the final day devoted to Interpretation, so spend as long as you wish practicing your Interpretation methods before moving ahead into the Application section. Below are a few topics you might want to consider.

Perhaps you still have questions concerning the importance of oaths (5:12). Are certain sects correct in refusing to "swear to God" even in a courtroom?

_____

_____

_____

Are we really supposed to resist becoming teachers (3:1)?

_____

_____

_____

God does not tempt anyone (1:13), yet He sometimes tests them (Genesis 22:1). Is there a significant difference between the two, or are we just splitting hairs?

_____

_____

_____

Have you reviewed the Old Testament stories James refers to?

- Abraham and Isaac (Genesis 22; James 2:21–24)
- Rahab (Joshua 2; James 2:25)
- Job (Book of Job; James 5:11)
- Elijah (1 Kings 17–18; James 5:17–18)

As you can see, there may be much left to be covered. And perhaps you wish to add other topics of your own for follow-up.

BOOK OF JAMES
Day 21

When it comes to Application, perhaps no book is easier than James to understand and start applying in numerous practical ways. Therefore, let's examine one chapter at a time, using the nine-question method to find as many ways as possible to begin to apply what James is telling us. Today's assignment is to read James 1 and answer these questions.

---

(1) Is there an example for me to follow?

(2) Is there a sin to avoid?

(3) Is there a promise to claim?

(4) Is there a prayer to repeat?

(5) Is there a command to obey?

(6) Is there a condition to meet?

(7) Is there a verse to memorize?

(8) Is there an error to mark?

(9) Is there a challenge to face?

BOOK OF JAMES
Day 22

Moving on to James 2, here are the same nine questions to consider. Remember, this is no longer a mere Bible "study." The purpose at this stage is Application. What are you finding in the text that should literally change the way you are living your life?

(1) Is there an example for me to follow?

(2) Is there a sin to avoid?

(3) Is there a promise to claim?

(4) Is there a prayer to repeat?

(5) Is there a command to obey?

(6) Is there a condition to meet?

(7) Is there a verse to memorize?

(8) Is there an error to mark?

(9) Is there a challenge to face?

BOOK OF JAMES
Day 23

Today, move on to the third chapter of James. After you finish answering the questions, be sure to give them some thought. This type of exercise can become a matter of putting words on a page unless we activate our hearts and minds during the process.

---

(1) Is there an example for me to follow?

(2) Is there a sin to avoid?

(3) Is there a promise to claim?

(4) Is there a prayer to repeat?

(5) Is there a command to obey?

(6) Is there a condition to meet?

(7) Is there a verse to memorize?

(8) Is there an error to mark?

(9) Is there a challenge to face?

BOOK OF JAMES
Day 24

Today we come to James 4. You know what to do by now.

___

(1) Is there an example for me to follow?

(2) Is there a sin to avoid?

(3) Is there a promise to claim?

(4) Is there a prayer to repeat?

(5) Is there a command to obey?

(6) Is there a condition to meet?

(7) Is there a verse to memorize?

(8) Is there an error to mark?

(9) Is there a challenge to face?

BOOK OF JAMES
Day 25

Today you finish out the book of James (chapter 5) with your list of Application questions. When you finish, think back over your responses of the last five days. Spend some time meditating on the portions of James you want to commit to memory. See if you find any patterns or repetitions you hadn't yet noticed. Is James's purpose for writing becoming even clearer as you begin to apply what he was saying?

---

(1) Is there an example for me to follow?

(2) Is there a sin to avoid?

(3) Is there a promise to claim?

(4) Is there a prayer to repeat?

(5) Is there a command to obey?

(6) Is there a condition to meet?

(7) Is there a verse to memorize?

(8) Is there an error to mark?

(9) Is there a challenge to face?

BOOK OF JAMES
Day 26

By now you should have a good start in understanding how the content of James can be applied to your own life. You've gone straight through the book and have noted applications as they arise. Now let's reverse the process. Let's begin with a topic for Application and then see how James addressed that topic. If you've begun to understand James's culture, as well as your own, you should be able to create some Bible-based principles that apply to your life.

Today we'll begin with a simple one. See what James had to say about the topic of our speech. What applications and principles can you find that could guide you in the way you choose your words?

The next few days will deal with other topics that may not be quite as obvious, yet you should have no trouble finding numerous applications from the text of James.

Applications That Address Our Speech Habits

_____
_____
_____
_____
_____
_____

Principles to Live By

_____
_____
_____
_____
_____
_____

BOOK OF JAMES
Day 27

Today, examine the book of James and focus on what you can apply to your life about the topic of social status. Look for both specific applications and more general principles. Take into account that some two thousand years have passed since James wrote his letter. Make any necessary adjustments to adapt his instructions to your own culture.

Applications That Address Social Status

_____

_____

_____

_____

_____

_____

Principles to Live By

_____

_____

_____

_____

_____

_____

BOOK OF JAMES
Day 28

Currently, one of the most popular topics for books, talk shows, and daily conversations is spirituality. Everyone seems to have a different insight or opinion that will lead to deeper truth—whether or not it has anything to do with what the Bible has to say.

Your assignment today is to see what James said about religion and spiritual habits. What, specifically, did he expect of his readers? And what principles to live by can you formulate based on his writing?

Applications That Address Our Spiritual Habits

_____

_____

_____

_____

_____

_____

Principles to Live By

_____

_____

_____

_____

_____

_____

BOOK OF JAMES
Day 29

As you wind down your Bible study of James, we hope you're accumulating a lot of help and information that you can carry with you throughout your life. So far, we've been doing a lot of looking backward to see what James had to say, and then bringing relevant applications to the present. Today we want to look into the future. Though he placed less emphasis on this than on other topics, James did challenge us to take care in how we plan for the future. Your challenge today is to see how much you can find on this topic.

Again, take note of anything specific he said on the issues. Then create general principles that will be helpful and easy to remember.

Applications That Address Planning for the Future

_____

_____

_____

_____

_____

_____

Principles to Live By

_____

_____

_____

_____

_____

BOOK OF JAMES
Day 30

Perhaps this is the page you've been waiting for. It's the last activity in this workbook. However, we hope that this won't be an end for you, but rather a beginning. If you've learned the Bible study methods you've been practicing in this workbook, they should serve you faithfully in many, many studies to come.

As you close your study of James, we're going to leave this final day up to you. Look for an area of desired life change that you don't feel has been adequately addressed to this point, and meditate on what James has to say about it. We haven't said much about sickness, suffering, temptation, and other topics found in James. Whatever you choose, use the space below to list some specific steps you might take to heed what James was saying in order to make your life better from this point on.

_____

_____

_____

_____

_____

_____

_____

_____

_____

_____

_____

Supporting Resources from Howard Hendricks & Moody Publishers

Living By The Book

THE VIDEO KIT

Let the Bible come alive for you!
Dr. Howard Hendricks will show you a simple proven process for discovering and applying biblical truth for yourself.

This Video Kit includes

- **2 VHS videocassettes**

- **Companion Users Guide**

- ***Living By the Book*** **best-selling book from Moody Press**

- **7 sessions, 25 minutes each**

ISBN: 0-8024-9533-8

Observation [sessions 1-2-3]
Why don't people study the Bible - and why we must. Paying attention to terms, structure, literary form and atmosphere. Learning to look at the text - and look again! And learning what to look for!

Interpretation [sessions 4-5]
Five keys to understanding the text: content, context, comparison, culture and consultation of other biblical passages.

Application [sessions 6-7]
Teaches the vital importance of applying biblical truth and introduces a four-step process when applying scripture: know, relate, meditate and practice. Plus eight questions to ask any passage of Scripture.

MOODY
PUBLISHERS

THE NAME YOU CAN TRUST.

1-800-678-6928 www.MoodyPress.org

Moody Press, a ministry of the Moody Bible Institute,
is designed for education, evangelization, and edification.
If we may assist you in knowing more about Christ
and the Christian life, please write us without obligation:
Moody Press, c/o MLM, Chicago, Illinois 60610.